THE
PUPPY
EXPRESS

THE
PUPPY
EXPRESS

On the road with 25 dogs . . .
what could go wrong?

David Rosenfelt

sphere

SPHERE

First published in Great Britain in 2014 by Sphere
First published in the United States in 2014 by St Martin's Press

Copyright © 2013 by David Rosenfelt

The moral right of the author has been asserted.

A CIP catalogue record for this book
is available from the British Library.

ISBN 978-0-7515-5352-9

Printed and bound in Great Britain by
Clays Ltd, St Ives plc

Papers used by Sphere are from well-managed forests
and other responsible sources.

MIX
Paper from
responsible sources
FSC® C104740

Sphere
An imprint of
Little, Brown Book Group
100 Victoria Embankment
London EC4Y 0DY

An Hachette UK Company
www.hachette.co.uk

www.littlebrown.co.uk

This book is dedicated to Debbie Myers,
on behalf of thousands of dogs.

Acknowledgments

There are countless people to thank for supporting Debbie and me in our rescue efforts, and many of them are mentioned in this book. I apologize to those who are not.

I did want to make special mention of the amazing veterinarians and their staffs that have cared for our dogs along the way. Believe me, we are excellent judges of vet care, and these people are as good as it gets.

Lakeview Veterinary Clinic, Rockland, ME
Dr. Daniel Dowling
Christine Annis
Sue Luce
Debra Drake
Patty Mulholland

Acknowledgments

North Tustin Veterinary Clinic, Tustin, CA
Dr. Karuppana Kali
Terry Ryan
Julie Pantoja
Ardell McNay

Bay Cities Veterinary Hospital, Marina Del Rey, CA
Dr. Thomas Fitzpatrick
Dr. Mary J. Brandt
Dr. Sandy Milo

I'd also like to thank the terrific people at St. Martin's Press, including but not limited to Andy Martin, Daniela Rapp, Kelley Ragland, Hector Dejean, Joan Higgins, Paul Hochman, Lauren Hesse, Sarah Jae-Jones, Chesalon Piccione, and Elizabeth Lacks.

And of course, nothing would happen without the amazing Robin Rue, my agent at Writer's House.

THE
PUPPY
EXPRESS

Prologue

François de La Rochefoucauld wrote in 1650 that "the only thing constant in life is change."

I cite that quotation for two reasons. First, I believe it makes me the only author ever to begin a book with the words "François de La Rochefoucauld."

James Patterson, eat your heart out.

Second, if the eloquent Frankie R. were still around today, he would point at me and say, "You may have overdone it."

I moved to Southern California from New York twenty years ago. I had spent my entire working life as a marketing executive in the movie business. Except for a few mediocre advertising copy lines, I had never written a word that was published, nor one ever spoken by an actor or actress.

It wasn't that my prose had been rejected; I basically hadn't written anything, and I really didn't have much interest in doing so.

But if you're reading this book, and I'm figuring that there's a good chance you are, then you're reading the seventeenth book I've had published in the last ten years. The previous sixteen have been novels, including eleven in the Andy Carpenter series.

I've also had a bunch of my scripts produced as TV movies. Admittedly they are nothing that has changed American culture as we know it, but people have been able to turn on their televisions and watch my words attempt to entertain them.

So careerwise, I've changed enough to make François de La Rochefoucauld proud.

As the last decade of the twentieth century began, my life was set up as I liked it. I expended very little physical energy beyond the occasional game of racquetball, and I was happy to take it easy. I was writing, which should never be confused with manual labor, and doing so on my own schedule.

I appreciated my life of relative leisure, and I was determined to maintain it in all areas. For instance, while I liked dogs, I didn't have one and certainly had no plans to get one. I didn't want to invest the time and effort necessary to care for an animal; as a newly single guy, I could barely care for myself.

Fast-forward to now, and my wife, Debbie Myers, and I have twenty-five dogs. It's a relatively low number when taken in context of the last seventeen years. It's an extremely high number when taken in context of sane human behavior. It certainly represents a small percentage of the four thousand dogs we have saved.

While I had ultimately made a conscious decision to become a writer, the dog rescue thing just seemed to happen. Not so for Debbie. When she sets her mind to something and focuses on a goal, she doesn't rest until it's accomplished.

She's a force of nature, and when she made it her mission to save as many dogs as possible, I was just sort of swept along in the draft.

I've long resisted writing about our rescue work and our life with dogs, even though I'm always asked many questions about it at speaking engagements and book signings. Living it seemed sufficient.

But one day we found ourselves about to embark on something that motivated me to put fingers to keyboard. We were heading back East, not to New York but to Maine, and the dogs were of course coming with us.

So this is the story of our insane trip into dogland, and our equally insane trip to Maine. I have interspersed stories about special dogs that have touched our lives, and special situations that few humans are nutty enough to deal with.

One other point, on which I ask your indulgence: in certain cases when I don't know whether a dog is male or female, I'll use the word "it" when referring to that dog. This is not a sign of disrespect; I certainly don't think of dogs as objects. It's simply that it is cumbersome to always say "he or she."

With that out of the way, I present to you our unusual family.

Our very unusual, very large, very hairy family.

Dread and More Dread . . .

We were going on a journey that I expected would end up somewhere between that of Lewis and Clark and that of the Donner Party. Someone once said that the difference between an ordeal and an adventure is attitude. That's how I knew I was in for an ordeal.

We were eleven mostly intrepid travelers, closing the traditional exploration circle by heading east from Southern California to Maine. No wagons, just three RVs. After all, this is the twenty-first century.

Of course, we didn't have many of the difficulties that the early pioneers had to endure. They were going through uncharted territory; we'd MapQuested the route and had three GPSs to make it foolproof. They had limited rations; we had refrigerators full of food, and stoves and microwaves with which to cook it. Not that we were without our refreshment challenges; for instance, we'd have to use a manual corkscrew for the wine.

Their communications went as far as their voices could carry; we were loaded down with cell phones, BlackBerries, and iPads. One of our group said that we actually had more computer power on board than astronaut Alan Shepard did when he first went into space, but I have no idea if that's true.

One thing we shared with our predecessors was the presence of plenty of animals. Their animals were crucial to their trip, but ours were the very reason for our journey.

Their animals represented the transportation itself; the horsepower behind the vehicles was alive and breathing. They probably also provided food, but I'd just as soon not go there. But if the pioneers hadn't had the benefit of their horses, when we talk about going out west today, we'd mean Cleveland.

In our case, three gas-fueled RV engines were our power source. The animals were the passengers; we were transporting our dogs, all twenty-five of them, to our—and their—new home. They were all rescue dogs, a small portion of the thousands that we have saved from the misery of the Los Angeles shelter system, but this trip was likely to make new demands on their endurance.

Our group included nine other people that volunteered for the trip, which was pretty remarkable. Some were friends; others were readers of my novels whom I'd met only once or twice. Three of them I'd never met at all. Giving us their time and energy in this way was amazingly generous, and I planned to thank them four or five thousand times before we got to Maine.

Of course, at the time I was thinking "if" we got to Maine.

The truth was, this undertaking could have been even more daunting. Twenty-five is pretty much the fewest dogs Debbie and I have had in the last ten years. We've had as many as forty-two, but we feel that more than forty is slightly eccentric.

The human members of our team, none of whom had known

each other previously, had been corresponding by e-mail for weeks. They were totally enthusiastic. They seemed to regard this as an incredible adventure, destined to be a source of great memories for years to come.

Not me.

Since I've always been an "RV half empty" sort of guy, I expected it to be torturous at best, and a disaster at worst.

Which brings me to the obvious question: how the hell did we get into this situation?

It Began with Tara

Well, more accurately with Tara's mother, Debbie Myers. On September 26, 1992, we went out on a blind date to the movies, fixed up by a mutual friend, Cheryl Wlodinger. We saw Billy Crystal's *Mr. Saturday Night,* but, rebels that we are, we saw it in the late afternoon.

At the end of the film I flashed my most winning smile and asked Debbie if she wanted to go to dinner. She declined, saying that she had to go home to administer eye medicine to her dog.

Based on that response, I had a hunch that the heretofore irresistible Rosenfelt charm had not yet reached its full effectiveness. Fortunately, she saved me from an insecurity crisis by subsequently agreeing to go home and deal with the medicine, and then meet me at the restaurant.

Her round-trip would take forty-five minutes, and though the dinner would have delayed the medicine-giving by only a couple of hours, she didn't want to wait. Her dog had an eye infection; she needed the care, and she needed the care on time. It seemed strange, and a bit suspicious.

As it turned out, the eye medicine story was real, and I was soon to find out that Debbie was simply a lover of animals to a rather abnormal level.

Since we didn't talk much during the movie and drove to the restaurant separately, we knew almost nothing about each other when we finally sat down to dinner. I barely had time to start displaying my killer personality when the waiter came over to tell us the specials. They began with a veal chop.

Debbie cut him off with "We don't eat veal," and when he left, she launched into a spirited dissertation on the cruelty that goes into the preparation of that particular meat. I was so clueless that I didn't even know what animal veal came from, so I silently figured she perhaps had a pet veal at home to go with her eye-sick dog.

But her feelings about the matter were not the point. Who was she to decide what I would or wouldn't eat? I could have whatever the hell I wanted. It turned out that I wanted pasta, and by an amazing coincidence, I haven't wanted veal in the twenty years since we sat in that restaurant.

Debbie and I hit it off pretty well and found we had plenty to talk about beyond our shared disdain for veal. It was on our third date that I met her golden retriever, Tara, whose eye infection by then was just a memory. This kicked off a series of dates on which we would take Tara for walks, to the park, to the beach. She would go pretty much wherever we went.

That was the beginning of our love story, and things were also going well between Debbie and me. It wasn't long before her adoration of Tara didn't even seem so over the top; this truly had to be the best dog in the history of the world. And my insecurity about the delayed dinner was long gone; if Tara needed eye medicine, I would have left Heidi Klum to make sure that she received it.

Tara possessed a sensitivity that most humans don't even bother aspiring to. She had a built-in mood sensor, which enabled her to be sympathetic when Debbie or I was upset, playful when we were feeling good, affectionate when we needed it, and always—I mean always—ready to accept petting. She brightened up every room, park, or beach she visited.

She had her quirks, but like everything else about her, they were adorable. She loved biscuits but would never give us the satisfaction of seeing her eat one. Instead she'd let it lay there, feigning indifference, until we left the room. When we came back it was invariably gone, with only a few telltale crumbs as evidence. And the smug look on her face said, "I won again."

We had a certain walk we'd take her on that was probably her favorite. But when we were passing a house where she knew a particular German shepherd lived, she would stop cold, refusing to take another step. This was true even when the other dog was nowhere to be found.

We'd have to pick her up and carry all eighty-five pounds of her the fifty feet until we were past the house, at which point we'd put her down and she'd happily continue the walk. I don't think she was afraid; I think it was just a game she was playing with us. A game she never lost.

Tara was eight when I met her, and nine on the awful day that her nose started to bleed while we were taking a walk in Beverly Hills. We rushed her to the vet, who said it was either a foxtail caught in her sinus cavity or nasal carcinoma. If it was the latter, and that was what he suspected, it would "result in her demise."

He sent us to a surgeon, who confirmed the dire diagnosis. We authorized him to operate on her, even though we understood that there was no possibility it would save her life. We did it because he told us that it would give her more time, and there was pretty much nothing we wouldn't have done to get more time with Tara.

She came through the operation well, even if we didn't. Debbie told me that the night of the surgery was the first that Tara had ever spent out of the house. Debbie had once turned down a fantastic job opportunity in London because to have taken it would have meant that Tara would have been subject to that country's six-month quarantine policy. Such a thing would have been incomprehensible.

We brought Tara home two days after the operation. The surgeon admonished us not to let her get excited, or her nose would start to bleed. So when Debbie came home from work, she would park at the bottom of a three-block hill to prevent Tara from hearing her car. Then she'd sneak in and be in full petting mode before Tara even knew what hit her.

Tara lived three months after that, a period in which she was never alone, not even once, not for a minute. Medically, and quasi-medically, we tried everything, including such things as acupuncture and sprinkling shark cartilage in her food. The literature cited as evidence of the latter's effectiveness the fact that sharks never got cancer, a claim I was never able to confirm. But we tried it, because we would have done anything that had the slightest chance of success, so long as it did not affect the quality of whatever life Tara had left.

We took her on vacation to Carmel and stayed in Doris Day's dog-friendly hotel. We went to Zuma, Tara's favorite beach in Malibu, three times a week. But she gradually started to slow down; walks were becoming shorter, and her breathing was becoming heavier and more labored. While both Debbie and I noticed it, neither of us would admit it, and Tara's occasional good days provided sustenance to our denial mechanism.

Tara's appetite also diminished gradually until finally she was refusing food. We discovered that hot dogs were the one thing she could not resist, so we grilled them twice a day. It was foolish on our part, and we've gotten wiser since. Tara was telling us that it was time to go, and we were trying to create reasons for her to stay. Just for a little while longer.

Debbie was having a lot of trouble dealing with her emotions during this time. Her vet recognized this and put her in touch with Marilyn Bergman, who, along with her husband, Alan, is an extraordinarily successful songwriter. They had been through the loss of their dog, and the vet thought that Marilyn could be helpful.

She certainly was. She talked to Debbie about the need to let go, for Tara's sake. She described her own, similar experience, and it definitely had an effect on Debbie.

Soon after, the day finally came when we couldn't fool ourselves anymore. We took Tara to the park for a picnic, and she wouldn't eat, not even the cherished hot dogs. We also noticed that she would not sit in the sun; obviously her condition had expanded to include an aversion to bright light.

We took her directly from the park to the vet, and he got right to the point. "I'm sorry, but it's time."

It's very hard for me to convey how I felt at that moment. It was as if a train had been slowly bearing down on us, and though we saw it coming months in advance, we just couldn't seem to get out of its path. The sadness was unbearable, oppressive; it seemed as if we were suffocating.

We felt as if we had let Tara down. She was depending on us—we were the only chance she had—and we hadn't come through. She deserved so much more, but we just couldn't seem to give it to her.

But whatever guilt and grief we were experiencing, the bottom line was that the vet was right, and none of the other stuff mattered anymore.

It was time to let Tara go.

He put two blankets on the floor, double thickness so they would be softer, and Tara laid down on them. Debbie and I both got on the floor with her, a position we have assumed with many other dogs since.

We held her while the vet gave her an injection, which was a sedative designed to calm her, though she really didn't need calming. She was peaceful and accepting.

He shaved her leg above her vein and administered the pink liquid. She didn't react to anything he was doing; she just stared into Debbie's eyes, silently saying good-bye.

I swear, she looked at us with a level of dignity and courage that only golden retrievers possess and told us that it was OK.

And it was.

We stayed with her, alone in the room, for at least fifteen minutes after it was over. I don't think a word was spoken the entire time.

When we finally got up and left, Debbie and I went back to the Malibu beach that Tara loved so much, and we sat there and took turns crying and consoling each other. I tried to focus on the consoling, since she had known Tara for nine years, while I'd had the pleasure for only one.

It would be a while before we fully realized what a transforming experience the past three months had been. Our lives would never be the same; we would soon embark on a mission that could fairly be described as dog lunacy.

But at that moment, all we could focus on was the oppressive sadness that we felt. We talked about things Tara had done, quirks in her behavior, and how much we loved her. We decided in the moment that neither of us would ever eat a hot dog again, as a way of honoring her.

At this writing it's a vow we have kept for twenty years, even extending the ban to pigs in a blanket. As someone who grew up with the idea that a great meal could be enjoyed while standing at the counter at Nathan's in Coney Island, I confess that I wish Tara had instead had a preference for broccoli in those final days.

Debbie and I would find ourselves laughing at some memory, but the laughter was short-lived. It was just so hard to process the knowledge that Tara had died.

Except she hadn't.

Not really.

We would see to that.

A Really Long Year

In one crucial way, Debbie and I reacted very differently to losing Tara. I was ready to get another dog right away—a golden retriever, to be exact. But Debbie couldn't bring herself to do it; she seemed to shut herself off from even considering the possibility.

Every dog she saw reminded her of Tara, but no dog could ever be Tara. And certainly no dog could ever replace her.

So instead of taking walks with a dog around our Santa Monica neighborhood, we would just be two humans out for a stroll. The problem was that I think there are more goldens on a per capita basis in Santa Monica than anywhere in the world; having a golden must be a town ordinance or something.

Every time Debbie would see one, which meant at least once on every block, she would start to cry. And I'm not talking about eyes filling with tears and getting choked up. I'm talking about full-blown sobbing, right there on the street.

It's fair to say that our walks were not something I looked forward to.

A friend suggested that we might get some comfort from volunteering at an animal shelter, and I was enthusiastic about the idea. My hope was that it would get Debbie comfortable with dogs again and maybe even pave the way toward our getting one. I think she had some trepidation, but she went along.

We went to the West Los Angeles shelter for an orientation meeting. It's one of the better shelters in Los Angeles County, but that is bestowing faint praise, since the other ones are, in varying degrees, disasters.

The staff started the meeting by telling the apocryphal story of a guy walking on a beach where thousands of starfish had washed ashore and would die if not quickly returned to the water.

He began picking up the starfish one at a time and tossing them into the water. Another man came up to him and pointed out that with so many thousands of stranded starfish, he was wasting his time and effort. There was no way that one person could make a difference.

The man responded by picking up another starfish and returning it to the water. "I made a difference to that one," he said.

The point was that even though the Los Angeles shelter system is overwhelmed by the sheer volume of abandoned animals, we could make a difference by focusing on saving one animal at a time. It made sense to us, so we signed on.

We should have stuck with the starfish.

We reported dutifully for work two evenings a week and a full day on Saturday. We also took dogs to mobile adoptions in shopping centers, waiting for people to come by, fall in love, and take one home.

But there were too many great dogs and not enough decent potential owners. So we had to sit in the overcrowded shelter, watching as dogs languished in cages until some of them were euthanized so that others could take their place. We also had to watch as people came in and adopted animals to use as guard dogs, or worse.

As bad as that was, it's not what pushed us over the edge. One day we were in a shelter in Baldwin Park that made the West LA shelter look like the Ritz-Carlton. A guy came in with his three sons and their one-year-old Lab mix. As we listened, the idiot explained to the shelter worker that they were turning the dog in; they didn't want it anymore.

He was given a standard form to sign, acknowledging that he had been told his relinquished pet could be put down after one hour. This wouldn't really happen, at least not that fast, but the truth was that owner turn-ins to that shelter did not last long at all. If a dog is found stray, it has to be kept for at least five days, to give the owner time to show up and claim it. But when the owner turns it in voluntarily, there is no such need, and the amount of time the dog will live is dependent on how overcrowded the shelter is at that particular time. The Baldwin Park shelter, it should be noted, was always over-crowded.

So the man casually signed the paper, and as the worker went to process it, Debbie and I overheard his conversation with his sons. It seemed they had adopted the dog from the same shelter ten months earlier, when it was a puppy. Now that it was full grown, they didn't want it anymore, because puppies were cuter.

So they were getting rid of it, without apparent regret or embarrassment, and then going into the kennel area to find another puppy to adopt. And the shelter rules for LA County made it a perfectly legal thing to do.

I was outraged, but Debbie lost it. She berated the man, calling him an asshole. She probably shouldn't have done so in front of his kids, though they would eventually find out that her description was accurate, if they didn't know it already. My natural aversion to confrontation kicked in, and I stood off to the side, pretending I didn't even know what was going on.

The man backed off, the first wise thing he had done in probably ever, and they left without getting a new dog. I'm sure it was a temporary victory; they most likely came back when they were certain Debbie wasn't on the premises.

We told the shelter workers that if the turned-in dog was not adopted, we'd find a rescue group to take it, and we eventually did so.

And then we bailed out of there, and out of the shelter system as well. If we were going to make a real difference, it would have to be another way.

And it wasn't long before we found one.

The Endless Planning

We'd known that we were going to be moving east, with all the dogs, for five years.

Ever since the fire.

In the summer of 2000, we moved from Santa Monica south to Orange County, because Debbie took a job down there as a vice president in charge of media at the Taco Bell corporation, based in Irvine. She had been a senior vice president at the FOX television network for twelve years, so it was a big move, both careerwise and, to a lesser extent, geographically.

Normal people could just find a place, sign up to buy or rent, pack up their things, and move. But we were not exactly a normal family. We had to find a home that could house thirty-seven dogs, since that was the total at that particular moment. We also couldn't have nearby neighbors, for reasons that are obvious but that I'll explain in detail later. So house hunting became something of a challenge.

As we were soon to discover, Santa Monica was the only city in Southern California that allowed more than three dogs per household. Santa Monica actually had no limit at all; their rule was that you could have as many animals as you could comfortably house. Comfort, I can assure you, was and is a subjective determination.

So when we got to Orange County, we were obligated to look in what they call the unincorporated areas, meaning they have no city government and are run by the county. We quickly found a perfect house in a small canyon town called Silverado. We were up on a hill, with very few neighbors within barking distance.

Even though it felt like living in the middle of nowhere, it was only ten minutes from a supermarket, and twenty from large shopping centers. The house was a hundred years old, but it would feel a lot older once it had to put up with our "family" for a while.

It proved to be quite comfortable for us, and we had every intention of staying there until Debbie might decide to retire. With that prospect nearing, I set out in September 2007 to figure out where we should move to once there was no job keeping us in California. I could write anywhere.

Debbie and I had both grown up and lived back east, me in New Jersey and then New York, and Debbie in Pennsylvania and New York. We craved real weather, and we have grown kids in the New York area, so the East Coast was the likely place to move.

We settled on Maine, found a great house on a lake with no neighbors anywhere close, and bought it. The plan was to let it sit there, and do whatever renovations might be necessary when we got ready to move. We figured that would be at least four or five years away.

One month later, California was in flames. There were wildfires all over the state, the by-product of a weather phenomenon

called the Santa Ana winds. These are winds that blow from in-
land toward the coast, and they are distinguished by very high
gusts, temperatures in the mid-nineties, and almost no humidity.
Obviously that creates the perfect conditions for out-of-control fires,
and that's what seems to happen every year.

With the state's firefighting resources taxed to the limit, some
moron decided to set a fire in the woods about six miles from our
house. At first it spread in the opposite direction, but three days
later it looped back toward us.

One morning I stood in our backyard and watched the fire
slowly coming across the canyon toward where I was standing. It
was small and slow-moving and therefore beyond infuriating; firefighters armed with water pistols could have stopped it in its tracks.

But there were no firefighters there; they were deployed
elsewhere. And the fire kept coming inexorably closer, building in
intensity.

Debbie was at work, and I called to tell her to come home; we
were likely going to have to evacuate. Our neighbors had already
gone, but for them it was comparatively easy. All they had to do
was round up some important possessions and ride out of there.
We had twenty-seven dogs to worry about.

We had one SUV at home, and Debbie went to a rental-car
place and got another. The fire was picking up speed even more rapidly, and I told her to get home as soon as possible; we were running
out of time.

There were police barricades not letting anyone into the area
when she arrived, but that didn't prove a significant deterrent.
She went around them and barreled on home, probably making
the correct assumption that what she was doing was not a shooting
offense.

We then began the process of loading the dogs and one duffel bag into the two cars. I think there were maybe three dogs willing and able to jump in on their own; the rest had to be hoisted once we rounded them up. I did the rounding, and Debbie did the hoisting.

We did a final count, and came up with twenty-six; Coco was missing. I searched frantically for her while Debbie tried to keep the others calm, not an easy thing to do since they were squashed into two cars.

Finally I found Coco wandering on the property, grabbed her, and carried her to the car. I stuffed her in, and we were off.

There was not a square inch of unoccupied space in the cars. The flames were about a hundred yards away and moving in the direction of the house; we were going to get out, but there seemed no way it could survive. I remember turning to take a final look at it.

We called a friend named Ron Edwards, who ran the Irvine Animal Care Center, one of the best shelters in Southern California. He said he had room to take and care for as many dogs as we brought him. So that's where we headed.

We left twenty-five of them there, a gut-wrenching thing to do. We had gotten these dogs from shelters, and had made a solemn promise to them that they would never have to go back. Their new surroundings would be temporary and safe, but they had no way of knowing that. They would be in cages, also something we had told them would never happen again.

Once they were in the dog runs, Debbie and I went in to each one, petting them and vowing that they would not be there long. But the truth was we didn't know how long they would be imprisoned, or where they would go once we got them out.

We kept Louis and Hannah, both golden retrievers, to stay with us in a hotel. Unfortunately, we didn't have a hotel, and once we dropped the dogs off at the shelter, we made at least twenty calls to try to get a room somewhere. But with much of California evacuated in the various fires, there were no rooms to be had.

We finally got lucky; the Irvine Marriott had one room. Amazingly, even though the law of supply and demand said that they could have charged a fortune, they gave us the room at half price, which was their policy for people displaced by the fires. And they made an exception to their no pet policy; we could bring Louis and Hannah.

I have been a fan of Marriott ever since. They really stepped up when we needed them.

So there we were, living in the hotel and watching news reports to monitor the progress of the fire. Louis and Hannah were living it up; they got to go on plenty of leash walks, since there was no doggie door for them to trudge through on their own. And we were on the concierge floor, where free food was provided, so I could get them plenty of miniature meatballs. If they felt any concern for their twenty-five friends stuck in the shelter, they hid it well.

But for us it was a frustrating time, made more so by on-camera statements that Governor Schwarzenegger was making to the press. He was explaining California's inability to deal with the fires by bemoaning the perfect storm that had arisen, a combination of high heat, high winds, and dry air.

"Arnold," I would yell at the television, "THAT'S WHAT THE SANTA ANA WINDS ARE! AND THEY COME EVERY YEAR!" It would be like the mayor of Buffalo explaining that they couldn't effectively plow the streets because of a combination of low temperatures and precipitation. "THAT'S WHAT SNOW IS!"

One day became two, and two became four. We saw hints of the fate of our house on television; one reporter stood in front of a burned-down structure less than a quarter mile away. But even though we were extraordinarily pessimistic, there was no way to be sure since they wouldn't let us back into the area where the fires were still raging.

So the question became, what the hell were we going to do in the likely event that the house was gone? When you have twenty-seven dogs, you can't exactly rent an apartment. And even if there were possible solutions, we had no time. Our dogs were languishing in a shelter; we didn't even go to visit them for fear of getting them excited and then letting them down when we left them there again.

We would have to move to Maine, or at least I would. Debbie would be bicoastal until maybe she could find a comparable job back east. The house in Maine wasn't close to ready or livable; it was a log-cabin style that wasn't even fully winterized. But we would somehow deal with that; we had no other choice. If only we could figure out how to get there.

On our fourth night in the hotel I got an e-mail from a reader in Maryland, who asked if we were anywhere near the fires. She described herself as a dog rescue person, and was of course concerned about the dogs.

I wrote back and told her that I thought we'd lost the house and asked if she, as a dog person, had any idea how to transport twenty-seven dogs cross-country. She didn't, but she vowed to ask the question online and get some ideas.

Over the next forty-eight hours, I received 171 e-mails from strangers, most of them offering us their house on the way to Maine. If we were coming through Topeka, for instance, we could stay in someone's home, with twenty-seven dogs!

It was an amazing example of what is a remarkable subculture of dog people in America. They are in every city and state, *bound together by their common love of dogs. And it had just been demonstrated to us in a very powerful and touching way.*

On the seventh day after our evacuation, we were let back into the area, and we were amazed to discover that our house had survived. Firefighters had foamed the house down and mounted a successful defense of the structure, and we will be forever grateful to them. Other nearby homes had not been so lucky, and the entire area seemed charred.

Two days after that we were back in the house, the whole family, shedding and panting away. But it had started us thinking about how we were going to execute the move to Maine when Debbie retired. It would be a voluntary move then, but just as difficult.

That was almost five years ago, so in terms of the length of time it took to plan our trip, it made the D-day invasion look like a spur-of-the-moment decision. Unfortunately, the effectiveness of the planning was another matter altogether.

The way I figured it, we could have used another five years, minimum.

Charlie

When volunteers work at mobile pet adoptions, they are generally assigned a specific dog to sit with and care for. They are expected to introduce potential adopters to the dog and explain its appealing traits.

Debbie sat with a dog named Charlie at a mobile adoption in Century City for an entire day, getting increasingly annoyed as the hours went by and no one showed any interest in him. He was listed in the shelter records as an Australian shepherd mix, but there was really no way to know his breed. Charlie was a mutt, in the best sense of the word.

His age was also a total guess. Vets make the judgment by looking at the condition of a dog's teeth, but it's an inexact science in the best case, and especially so with shelter dogs. They've likely lived outside a good portion of their lives, and could have done things like chew on rocks. They've also rarely had their teeth cleaned. In Charlie's case, the guesstimate of his age was nine, which meant that he was going to be very difficult to place in a home.

So Charlie sat in Debbie's lap all day, blissfully unaware that his euthanasia date was approaching. By day's end, she had fallen in love with him, and had decided that there was no way she was going to put him back in a shelter cage. The idea that they might kill a healthy, wonderful dog like this seemed unfair to the point of being absurd. So we adopted Charlie ourselves and took him home.

The idea was better in theory than in practice.

The problem was that "home" was an apartment we had moved to on Ninth Street in Santa Monica, one in which dogs were prohibited. So Debbie called the landlord and gave him a poignant speech about a dog she had taken off "death row," and he relented. Debbie can pretty much convince anyone to do anything; by the time she got off the phone, the landlord had probably sworn off veal.

Charlie was ours.

And so was Phoebe, a husky mix we fell in love with the following week in the shelter. Her time was up, and we watched as a potential adopter debated for two days whether to take her, and ultimately decided not to. We could not bear to watch her die, so she became ours.

And so did Sophie, a nine-year-old golden retriever who re-defined sweetness in a dog, and who we were not about to let suffer in a shelter. In fact, when we arrived at the shelter that day and saw her there for the first time, I immediately took her out of the cage and announced to anyone who would listen that she was officially our dog.

And so was Harry, a Newfie/Lab mix who was hilariously psychotic—way too crazy and huge for anyone else to want.

So we had four large dogs in an apartment that didn't allow any, though we had dispensation for one. We decided to be sneaky about it. We'd take one dog at a time for a walk, sometimes going down the stairs, in off hours using the elevator. We smiled and chatted with anyone we met, never letting on that we had more than one dog and hoping they wouldn't notice or care.

If they did catch on, they didn't say anything, except for one tenant, who people called "Mr. Jack." He was in his seventies and completely blind, so I can only assume he could smell the difference between the dogs.

"They let you have that many here?" he asked, and we said that they did. He smiled and said, "Great."

I was the one who finally suggested we move. Football season was approaching, and halftime was simply not going to be long enough to walk each dog individually.

So we went looking for a house to rent, and we found a great place not too far from the apartment. We signed a lease that was silent about allowing pets; though the pets in that house would prove to be as far from silent as is possible.

In any event, we knew we had reached our limit. More dogs would be unmanageable; even the four that we had made the house feel small.

Four dogs were certainly more than enough.

One year later we had twenty-seven.

Pong the Dalmatian

The West Los Angeles animal shelter was our home base of sorts, and it was where we did most of our volunteer work. As I mentioned, while it's one of the better shelters in Los Angeles County, that's not saying much.

For the most part, the people who work there try hard to do what's best for the animals, but it's a tough assignment. They aren't given enough space, resources, or funding. So they do what they can.

One of the things they do is hold special adoption days, usually on the weekend, and they attempt to drum up publicity for them. They provide incentives for adoption, usually reduced costs, and there are giveaways for the kids.

The shelter is located off Bundy Drive in West LA, but it had the disadvantage of being behind other buildings, and therefore couldn't be seen from the street. This tended to discourage drive-bys from stopping in, though in some ways that can be a positive. It cuts down on spur-of-the-moment impulse adoptions, which often don't work out.

People who work with dog rescue organizations are overwhelmingly female, probably 90 percent in my experience. As one of the token males at the West LA shelter, I was given some of the unenviable assignments, and on one particular special adoption day, it was a beauty.

In order to attract passersby who couldn't see the shelter from the street, someone would dress up in a Disney-type animal costume and go out on Bundy Drive. On this day the costume was of Pong the Dalmatian, and the sucker they dressed up was yours truly.

The major disadvantage to the job, other than the fact that I looked and felt like a dope, was the midsummer heat. It was ninety-five degrees outside, which was chilly compared to inside the Pong suit. I felt charcoal broiled within five minutes of the time I put it on. I will never again say, "Get lost, creep," when approached by a character at a theme park.

But I dutifully went outside in my costume and started attracting attention. There was a traffic light on the corner, so I would approach stopped cars and go into my act.

I would get on my knees and assume the begging position, as though I were imploring people to come in and adopt a dog. I would dance like an idiot, wave my arms wildly, and do whatever else was necessary to get people to notice me. Because in Los Angeles, just dressing up as Pong the Dalmatian doesn't get it done.

And to a degree I succeeded, in that people definitely paid attention. They would point at me and laugh, yelling things and getting into the spirit. Kids were most enamored of me, and for the hour that I was out there, the Bundy traffic light was a fun place to be.

Except, of course, for me. Though no one could know it by looking at me, I was fully baked and miserable. You can't tell a fake Dalmatian by its cover.

But the really annoying part was that I was completely ineffective. While everyone was noticing me and was laughing both with me and at me, I wasn't getting people into the shelter. When the light turned green they would move on, leaving poor Pong behind. I wasn't, as they say, putting asses in seats.

So my time ended with my not having gotten a single person to come to the shelter who wasn't already going there. I went inside to peel off the suit, though by that point everything was so hot and melted that it was hard to tell where the suit ended and my skin began. I had probably lost ten pounds in that hour, which is to say that I should get a few Pong suits for my regular wardrobe.

There was one other sacrificial male lamb in the shelter, and he was tasked with going out as my replacement Pong. After my performance, he was going to have big rubber shoes to fill. On my suggestion, he hosed down the suit with cold water inside and out before putting it on, and after he did so, he asked, "Where's the sign?"

And then it hit me, as well as everyone within laughing distance of my discovery. There had been a sign prepared for us Pongs to carry and wave around, announcing ANIMAL ADOPTION DAY and directing people into the shelter.

I had forgotten to bring the sign outside with me, so people passing by had no idea what the hell I was doing out there. To them I must have been just an idiot in a Dalmatian suit, a humorous if bizarre diversion, but not an invitation to enter the shelter.

Ever sensitive, Debbie laughed the hardest at my humiliation, and was instrumental in "Pong" becoming my nickname for the remainder of our time at the shelter.

Hanging Up the Tacos

In July 2010, Debbie decided to retire. She informed her colleagues at Taco Bell and agreed to stay on until February 2011 to help in the transition.

The decision contained both positives and negatives for me—and after all, isn't it all about me? The overriding positive was that Debbie would be home, not working twelve-hour days. She'd worked hard her entire life, and now she'd get to do whatever she wanted, which included relaxing. And best of all, we would be free to move to Maine.

On the negative side, among Debbie's areas of responsibility at Taco Bell were sports media and sponsorships. As part of that, we went to virtually every big sporting event that interested me . . . every Super Bowl, World Series, All-Star game, et cetera.

We even used to go to all the BCS Bowl games; within three days we'd go to Miami for the Orange Bowl, New Orleans for the Sugar Bowl, and Phoenix for the Fiesta Bowl, and then a week *later we'd go to the championship game, wherever it might be held. And as the happy spouse, I had absolutely no responsibility at these events other than to smile and look pretty.*

There are worse ways for a sports degenerate like me to live.

But suddenly the die was cast. The move that I had been unsuccessfully planning for five years was soon to be upon us, and I still had absolutely no idea how to do it.

So I decided to get some opinions.

I sent a mass e-mail to every reader who had ever e-mailed me, and the number was well into the thousands. Then I posted on Facebook, asking everyone to please send me their ideas and to solicit suggestions from their friends.

I got in excess of four thousand responses. Mostly they were things that I had already thought of and planned to check out . . . planes, trains, buses, vans, horse trailers, RVs, et cetera.

Someone on Facebook said that since I had worked in Hollywood, I should get John Travolta or Oprah Winfrey to lend me their plane. This triggered a flurry of comments, most from people who thought it was a damn good idea. None of those commenters, unfortunately, was Mr. Travolta or Ms. Winfrey.

First I called the "pet airlines," so named because their sole function is to transport pets. Not only were they prohibitively expensive, but it just didn't feel right for our dogs. The way they did it meant that the trip cross-country involved quite a few stops, so many that the entire thing would take twenty-four hours.

The idea of our old dogs being away from us for so long did not sit well with Debbie or me, for a number of reasons. They would be terribly stressed out, and we didn't want to put them through it.

Plus, the amount of medication that they receive daily is mind-boggling. Eight of them are on pain meds for arthritis, both in liquid and pill form. We also have two epileptics, two suffering from incontinence, one with Cushing's disease, and never fewer than two with ear infections or some other ailment. Administering all of these meds is a major project, and I was afraid it wouldn't be handled correctly by anyone other than us. For instance, if handlers accidentally misidentified two dogs and switched their meds, it could be a disaster.

Since these were all dogs who had been abandoned prior to coming to live with us, we never wanted them to worry about that possibility again. Twenty-four hours in cages with strangers, shuttling on and off of airplanes, might make them fearful that we were gone from their lives for good. At least that's how our human minds figured it.

Additionally, the closest the airlines would leave them was Boston, which presented all kinds of other problems for us. So pet airlines were not going to work.

Next I tried the regular airlines. Continental told me that the cost of flying a dog one way was somewhere in the $450 range.

"We are a special case, so you might want to make an accommodation," I said. "We have twenty-five dogs. How much would it cost us to move all twenty-five?"

If the agent seemed surprised by the number, he hid it well. "Well, each one would be four hundred and fifty dollars."

"You might get some good publicity out of it," I said.

"I don't know anything about that," he said, and I certainly believed that he didn't.

In any event, this wasn't going to work either. We'd have to buy carriers for each of our dogs of a size that could cost two hundred dollars apiece. Then only one or two dogs could go on each flight, and we'd have to be at the airport each time to meet them.

And if we wanted to fly them nonstop, it would have to be Boston. The closer Portland airport would require switching planes.

The whole thing was way too expensive and unwieldy.

Nothing else seemed like it was going to work. Horse trailers aren't air-conditioned, cargo vans could not be rented one way, we didn't have enough drivers for rented SUVs, party buses were bizarrely expensive, and I was sure no RV rental company would be crazy enough to allow twenty-five dogs on their vehicles.

So I expanded my solicitation of ideas. I was doing a book tour the summer that Debbie decided to retire, so rather than bore my audiences with talk of my books, I spent time during my talks asking everyone how the hell we were going to get to Maine.

I went to Arizona to do signings in Tucson and Phoenix. When I arrived, it was 115 degrees in the sun. I'm not sure what the temperature was in the shade, because there is no shade in Arizona.

While driving to Tucson, I got caught in a monsoon. People, including me, will sometimes refer to a heavy rainstorm as a "monsoon," but that isn't technically accurate. This was actually and literally a monsoon, and it was unlike any rainstorm I had ever been in.

Then, on the drive back to Phoenix, I was caught in a haboob. That's the name they give to massive dust storms, as if a funny-sounding name will make them seem less awful. It doesn't work; this haboob was unbelievable and very frightening. It was fifty miles wide, and I would estimate that it reduced visibility on the highway to maybe six or seven inches.

The haboob that I was in actually made the national newscasts. It was surreal; the entire world turned dark, and when it was finished, the entire world was covered in dirt. It would remain that way, baking in the 115-degree heat, until another monsoon came and washed it away.

So when I got to the signing in Phoenix, I told everyone we were moving to Maine, and asked if anyone had any ideas on how to move the dogs.

They didn't, and spent most of the time expressing their amazement that we would move to Maine.

How, they asked, would we be able to stand the extreme weather?

The Tara Foundation

The only way to survive being in dog rescue in Southern California is to focus like a laser on the victories and block out the defeats. It's not an easy thing to do, since the number of defeats is simply overwhelming.

When you volunteer in a shelter, you try to get to know the individual dogs. That way you can provide them with affection and comfort, and you can also more effectively persuade potential adopters to take them.

The unhappy flip side is that getting to know them leads to loving them, which leads to terrible pain if they are subsequently euthanized, as so many are.

It's as if each dog has a clock attached to it, and the time remaining on that clock inexorably clicks down. If someone doesn't come in and adopt the dog before it gets to zero, then the dog will die. And the moment that time runs out is unpredictable; usually it's directly related to the number of other dogs that are turned in or found stray, and the previously available space that is therefore occupied.

The rescue problem in the Los Angeles animal control system is simply a function of supply and demand; there are many more great dogs than there are good homes that want them. A deficiency in spaying and neutering is obviously one of the causes, but that isn't nearly all of it. There are a great many people who possess what in my eyes is a disturbing mind-set toward animals. They view them as possessions, as discardable as a piece of furniture. Unfortunately, the law takes a similar position, though that is finally changing in many localities.

I've met plenty of dog owners who made me wish their own parents had been spayed and neutered.

One day my daughter, Heidi, was looking for a dog, and she went with us to a mobile adoption in Century City. There she met Gigi, a one-year-old Australian cattle dog mix who was pretty much as sweet as they come. They bonded instantly, and Heidi took her home that night.

Debbie and I met the woman who runs Perfect Pet Rescue, the group that saved Gigi and placed her with Heidi. Her name is Nancy Sarnoff, and she is as dedicated a rescue person as exists on the planet. Debbie and I talked with her for an hour, and by the time we left, we had come to a conclusion.

We could do this. We could start our own rescue group.

Debbie and I approached the task with slightly different viewpoints. For her it was a solution to her recently expressed desire to do more productive things outside of her job, and she relished the prospect. And if she could help animals in the process, all the better. Her commitment was total and instantaneous.

I had some concerns. For example, most adoptions are

done on weekends, which happens to be exactly when football
is on television. And this wasn't some down-the-road problem;
Labor Day was approaching.

As is the case close to 100 percent of the time, Debbie's
enthusiasm ran roughshod over my hesitancy and procrastina-
tion. We started with the name, which was the easy part. By
decree we announced that we were now running the Tara Foundation, dedicated to the rescue of abandoned and homeless dogs,
primarily golden retrievers.

There are no licenses necessary to establish a foundation
like this; all it takes is the willingness to do the work and care
for the dogs. We started with a couple of advantages. Rather
than go through the long process of securing a nonprofit tax
status, we became a subsidiary of Perfect Pet Rescue, thanks to
the amazing Nancy Sarnoff. Also, having volunteered in the
shelter system, we knew our way around it and had made some
important contacts.

The only real disadvantage was that it was just Debbie
and me, and she had a full-time job. Most rescue organizations have a large group of volunteers to draw on, but we did
not. We probably should have gone out of our way to recruit,
but we never did, and we wound up with only four part-time
volunteers the entire time we operated. They were a huge help,
especially a woman who was with us almost the entire time,
Cathy Pearl.

But Debbie and I wound up doing almost all the rescuing
and the walking and the advertising and the screening of potential adopters on the phone, and everything else. It was physically
and emotionally draining.

The one thing that was absolutely no problem was finding
the dogs to rescue. The shelter system was overflowing with

them, all types and all sizes; we just needed to figure out where to put them once we got them out of the shelters.

Sort of by definition, someone who would dump their dog in a bad shelter probably hadn't taken very good care of it anyway. So the dogs we would be saving might well have health issues that would need to be addressed. They'd also need a bath and shots, and a safe place to stay while we were finding them a home.

A vet's office would provide all of the above, and we soon discovered that they were eager to have us. All of those things cost money, and even though they offered us a generous discount, it was still very much in their interest to serve as our base of operations.

So in no time at all we had what we physically needed to get going.

Except for the dogs.

We started making the rounds of shelters, primarily looking for golden retrievers. Amazingly, they're not in short supply; we got eight of them immediately. But we soon realized that we could not and should not rescue only goldens; there were too many terrific, deserving dogs, both mixes and pedigrees, for us to limit ourselves.

We had the physical space at the vet's office to house twenty-five dogs at a time, and there was no reason to ever be below that number. We would take in all the golden retrievers that needed us and use the remaining space for other deserving dogs.

We'd do our shelter runs once or twice a week, depending on how adoptions were going. We had to go through the same process as anyone else, adopting each dog individually. Once we did that, we loaded up our cars with as many dogs as we had room for. We usually placed about twelve a week in homes, so that's how many new ones we were able to take.

Almost all of our adopters learned about us through ads in the *Los Angeles Times*. This was before the proliferation of the Internet, which today makes things much easier. Potential adopters can now go online and see and read about available dogs. They can also fill out pre-applications. I wish we'd had those things available to us back then.

It was a simultaneously exhilarating and horrible experience. On the one hand, it was the purest form of rescue. We were taking dogs that had no chance, and once we had them it was an ironclad guarantee that they would wind up in a good home.

But we were picking them from thousands of equally worthy animals, and we knew that only a small percentage of those we left behind would make it out. The animals we were looking at were the starfish, and like the man on the beach, we could make a difference to only a very, very small percentage.

That meant we were literally making life-or-death decisions, not something I would recommend to others. We'd walk by the dog runs in the shelters, and the dogs we'd pick out would live, and the ones we'd walk by would most likely die. And there was nothing we could do about it.

Ultimately, about 60 percent of the dogs we rescued were goldens, and the rest were mostly mixes. One thing that they had in common was their size; because smaller ones had a better chance of being adopted out of the shelter, we focused on large ones. It was rare that we took a dog under sixty pounds.

Things immediately went well, at least in terms of finding homes for the dogs. People are much more willing to deal with rescue groups than shelters, at least in Southern California. Just the idea of walking into a shelter is daunting for animal lovers. They fear that what they will see will break their hearts, and very often it will.

Dealing with a rescue group like ours removes that danger, and also provides security. Adopters had to sign a contract that obligated them to return the dog to us if the adoption didn't work out well, for whatever reason. That removed the chance of their having to take the dog back to a shelter, where returned dogs generally did not fare well. By bringing the dog back to us, they would know that it would be well taken care of, so the potential guilt factor was removed.

I should say that the guilt factor was removed from the adopter, but not from us. We chose dogs who appealed to us, and who seemed most in need. Very often, that need would make them less likely to be wanted by others.

So what happened was that we would rescue a dog and either know going in, or subsequently find out, that it possessed a quality that would make it virtually unadoptable to anyone else. Perhaps the dog was old or had epilepsy or bad hips or whatever. The majority of people, even well-intentioned ones, did not want to deal with issues like this.

A perfect example of this was Nugget, a ten-year-old golden that was dumped in the South LA animal shelter. Nugget had a seizure while in the shelter, which would almost assure his not getting adopted, especially with his advanced age.

But Nugget was also blind, which made it 100 percent certain that he was going to be euthanized. No one would deal with the expense and difficulty of taking Nugget into their home, not when there were healthy young dogs in the same shelter, even in the same run.

But there were few things more painful than seeing how scared Nugget was in that cage, not being able to see his surroundings and being picked on by the other dogs. There was simply no way we could leave him there, though we knew it would be fruitless to even put him up for rescue. So Nugget came home with us, and he lived two happy and safe years.

That happened frequently, and was the reason our home gang kept expanding. Our guilt instantly kicked in; once we rescued a dog, how could we just leave it in a cage at our vet, constantly being rejected by potential adopters? What kind of life was that? The dog would have been better off facing its fate in the shelters.

There was also a more practical consideration. If a particular dog occupied one of our cages for a lengthy period of time, then it cut down on the amount of new dogs we could bring in.

All of this left us with two options. We could either keep the dog in a cage while we failed to find him a good home or bring him to ours. We kept choosing the latter, and it surprisingly became easier, rather than harder, as the number in our house increased.

When you have two dogs, getting a third is a big decision. For instance, the vet costs increase by 50 percent. But when you have twenty-one, one more doesn't seem much of an additional hardship. And if you have twenty-eight, and a shelter calls and says that a twelve-year-old golden will be put down that afternoon if you don't come and get it, then you go and get it, and you raise your number to twenty-nine.

So dogs kept coming home with us, one after another after another. We had crossed over into full-blown dog lunacy and burned the bridge behind us.

Princess

Debbie and I were at a shelter in Downey, California, called SEACCA. It was an overcrowded, awful place, which is why we got many of our dogs from there. We wanted to get them from the shelters where they would have the least chance of otherwise being adopted.

It seems counterintuitive, but very often the worst shelters are run by the most caring people, and SEACCA was a perfect example of this. The shelter supervisor was Ron Edwards, who later became head of the Irvine shelter and provided our dogs sanctuary in the fires. At SEACCA, Ron did everything he could to protect the animals in his care. The fact that it was so often a losing effort did not change that simple fact.

One day Debbie and I were walking through SEACCA when we saw a kennel worker leading a dog, not with a leash, but at the end of a long pole. That pole, plus the room toward which they were heading, made it clear to us that this dog was about to be euthanized.

Intellectually, there was nothing shocking about it. We knew that euthanasia was very common there; a high percentage of the "inmates" never came out. For example, the public shelters in California reported euthanizing 391,000 dogs in 2007, and most observers believe that shelters tend to underreport. The scene that was playing out in front of us no doubt happened many, many times each day.

This particular dog was adorable, a terrier mix of some sort, no more than thirty pounds. She was getting up in age, and from a distance I would have guessed that she was maybe seven years old. Her fur was matted and dirty, but she had a smile on her face, and not a clue where she was going.

Except she wasn't going there for long.

They were maybe thirty feet from the euthanasia room when Debbie screamed, "WHERE THE HELL ARE YOU GOING WITH MY DOG?"

The man turned, as did probably everybody within a mile of where we were standing. What he saw was Debbie running down the hall toward him. She grabbed for the pole, and he was smart enough to let her have it. He looked so scared I thought he was going to give her his wallet.

Once she got the pole from him, she dropped it to the ground, ran over to the dog, and disconnected it from her collar. Then she picked her up, and she didn't put her down until we were in the car.

We took the dog, who Debbie named Princess, to the vet's office where we kept our rescue dogs. She was in good shape physically, so she soon became a candidate for adoption.

And once she was cleaned and groomed, she was even more adorable.

A couple in their mid-sixties showed up one day, along with their son, Richard. He was in his thirties and clearly had mental challenges. He spoke haltingly, without much affect; in the old, politically incorrect days we would have said he was "slow."

I had talked to the couple at length over the phone, so I knew that the man was a college professor at Cal State Fullerton, and that his wife did not work. She would be home most of the day with the dog that they'd adopt, and the dog would live and sleep in the house, an absolute requirement for us. But they hadn't mentioned their son.

They were interested in a golden retriever, but Richard had other ideas. He brightened when he saw Princess, and within three minutes he was sitting with her on his lap. He was smiling and petting her, and she was loving it. A bond had clearly been forged, and his parents made the adoption of Princess official. Life had turned around quite nicely for her.

It was about three weeks later when the husband called, with his wife on the extension. He asked that I have Debbie join the call as well, which she did.

From that point on, the wife did all the talking. She told us that Richard had been in an accident when he was six months old, and it had left him brain damaged. His behavior had been erratic ever since, to the extent that it became impossible for Richard to stay in their home full-time . . . he needed care at a special facility. For more than thirty years they had been able to take Richard only on weekends.

She went on to tell us that the transformation in Richard since they'd adopted Princess had been startling. She had a calming, pleasing effect on him. He doted on her, and since he was willing to be the doter, Princess was certainly of a mind to be the dotee. They were inseparable.

She told us that as a result, they had consulted with Richard's doctors, and all agreed that he could move out of the facility and in with them full-time. And he had done so that morning.

So they had called to say, "Thank you for giving us our son back."

I rarely tell this story at speaking engagements, because the memory of it chokes me up. The love of a dog had radically changed the lives of these three people for the better; it had brought a family together.

Princess had come in and done what medical science could not.

And one month earlier she had been on the end of a pole.

Duchess

I was doing a signing at Book Carnival near our home in Orange County, and near the end a woman came up to me to talk about a terrible situation she was facing. She said that her husband had cancer, and they couldn't have a dog around because of the possibility of infection. She said that they'd have to give up their ten-year-old black Lab, Duchess, and asked if I would take her.

The story she told didn't ring completely true for me, especially when I told her that I would take the dog, but that I would see myself as more of a caretaker for her. If the woman's situation changed, and it became OK for the husband to be in the house with Duchess, then she could take her back. She seemed uninterested in this possibility, which surprised me, because usually owners who are forced to give up their dogs for similar reasons grab on to the possibility of someday getting them back.

I really had no interest in dwelling on whether her story was accurate, because if she wanted or needed to give up this incredibly sweet dog, for whatever reason, then Duchess would probably be better off with us. But my suspicions increased in the two weeks after Duchess entered our home. I e-mailed the woman updates about her progress and how she was adapting that were very positive, yet she didn't respond.

The bottom line is that Duchess has now been with us for about four years, and she has never, not once, caused the slightest problem. She doesn't bark, she never gets angry, and when you walk by her, she rolls onto her back to get her stomach scratched. She's somewhat incontinent, but it's handled by medication. There could not be a nicer dog, and she's been a fantastic addition to our family.

Saint Cyndi

Four months before our trip was to begin, we still had no idea how we were going to do it. Travolta and Oprah had continued to selfishly withhold their planes, though I was staying by the phone just in case.

Debbie had the idea that maybe one of the cable networks would want to film the trip as a reality show, and they might therefore finance it and provide appropriate vehicles. I called a friend of mine who is a producer and active in that world to gauge the possibilities.

He said that the idea had potential, and that the trip might well be of interest, but there would be a few conditions that we would have to agree to. First of all, just a four- or five-day trip by itself wouldn't give a network nearly what it would need to fill a season, to say nothing of multiple seasons. They would have to set up shop in our house after we arrived, to document our day-to-day existence with the dogs.

That was bad enough; the chaos of a camera crew in our house with all the dogs was too horrible to even contemplate. To make matters worse, my friend said, the network would insist on "human conflict." Of course, if we were to do it, I'd be able to give them more than just conflict. I'd provide an on-camera suicide.

So we ditched the reality show idea.

No matter what method of transportation we ultimately chose, we had another problem that seemed insurmountable. We were going to need people to help us; there was no way around that. Debbie and I simply could not do it on our own.

I am not really the type to ask for a favor, and certainly not one of this magnitude. That's not to say I'm not a taker; I take with both hands. But I am not often an asker. And being a taker without being an asker is not an easy thing to pull off.

Enter Cyndi Flores.

I had communicated occasionally in the past with Cyndi, who had been living in North Carolina. She had e-mailed me, introducing herself and asking for my help with an auction her dog rescue group was having, so I donated a signed book and a character name. What that means is that the winning bidder could have his or her name used in a future book as a character. If they chose to, they could use their dog's name instead. I do that frequently with rescue groups around the country, and they often make pretty good money in the process.

The auction went well, and after that Cyndi and I communicated intermittently. I'm a hermit in real life but Mr. Sociable when it comes to e-mails. I had been impressed by Cyndi's dedication to the rescue group, and her obvious ability to make things happen.

So, since I had asked almost everybody else in America if they had ideas on how to move the dogs, I asked her. The next day she e-mailed me back, and her message included the following:

Potential Challenges Moving Dogs Cross-Country

1. Vehicles for 20+ dogs and humans to drive them.

2. Poop and exercise breaks (getting them out of vehicles, leashed, walked, etc.).

3. Feeding breaks and having to carry enough food or buy in transit.

4. Places to sleep dogs and humans comfortably.

5. Risk Management Plan—what to do if there are car problems, sick dogs, or other travel issues (traffic, accident, etc.).

6. Need to research state laws in the travel path to make sure there aren't any silly laws like you can't have 10 dogs in a Winnebago.

7. And I'm sure things I haven't even thought of yet.

This was too good to be true; Cyndi Flores was heaven-sent. And if I had any doubt about that, she further informed me that she wanted to join us on the trip, and thought she could recruit some friends to come along as well.

I didn't want to go overboard, so I offered her the position of Grand Exalted Empress of the Trip, and she accepted. My plan was that I would be the figurehead leader, the puppet, but she would be pulling the strings. It's a position I'm comfortable with.

Thus began a lengthy back-and-forth, probably a hundred e-mails in all, in which we brainstormed possible ideas. The mode *of transportation remained the biggest problem, and I decided to make as many calls as I could, to as many places as I could think of, to find out what our options really were. Cyndi was going to do the same.*

My first idea was to use trucks, since they're obviously large and would hold a lot of dogs. We could cover the floor with blankets and make it comfortable for them. I called Penske, Ryder, and every other truck company I could find, but none of them had trucks that were air-conditioned.

I politely declined, but they're not really the types to take no for an answer. Once you contact these companies, they pretty much call you back every twenty minutes to try and get you to take the offer you declined in the first place.

Horse trailers were the next option. A reader who works at Hollywood Park racetrack in LA was nice enough to do some research for me and discovered that they are no longer air-conditioned. There are open-air windows to keep things cool, but they are high up, because horses are tall. Only our mastiff, Wanda, would be comfortable in those conditions.

Trains didn't work for a bunch of reasons, but the main one was that there would be no way to walk the dogs. Twenty-five dogs in a closed car for five days could get a tad gamey.

I found some more companies that rented party buses, the kind that touring musicians might use. They were still way too expensive and wouldn't allow dogs on them anyway. We considered buying an old school bus and tearing out the seats, but I worried about having us all in one vehicle. If it broke down, as an old school bus on that kind of long trip might do, we'd be history.

The idea I was most hopeful about was to use cargo vans. They are roomy, and three vans might comfortably house all the dogs. Most important, they are open between the passenger section and cargo section, so the air-conditioning would circulate throughout. They aren't even that expensive to rent; we had used them on our relatively short move from Santa Monica to Orange County.

It seemed so perfect that there was of course no way it could work, and it didn't. No one would rent a cargo van one way; I think they were obeying some sort of edict designed to make our lives miserable. Cargo vans are rented only for short moves, maybe taking furniture from one place to another, and there were no exceptions that we could get anyone to make.

Next on the list were RVs, and we looked into buying a couple. Based on the price, we quickly dismissed that as insane, especially since we didn't want to have a driveway full of RVs at our house in Maine. Selling things like that privately is not our thing, and we didn't want to have to deal with it. When the trip was over, we wanted the trip to be over.

In my case, even before the trip began, I wanted the trip to be over.

I looked into renting RVs, but I felt I should be up front about the cargo they would be carrying. It didn't go over well with the one company I tried; they said that one dog would be fine, maybe two, but the number we were talking about was out of the question.

So Cyndi and I decided that we would keep digging and researching while simultaneously tackling another problem.

Regardless of what we were traveling in, where the hell would we sleep along the way?

Bumper

One of the best decisions I made when I started writing novels was to put my e-mail address in my books, openly inviting feedback. I quickly discovered that readers are basically nice and will write to an author only if they like the book.

The net result is that I have gotten almost exclusively positive responses, and when a new book comes out, I get thousands of e-mails from strangers, telling me how great I am.

As you might imagine, I have to fight off the desire to get up at three o'clock in the morning to check out the computer. One of the reasons I don't do so is that when I get back, there is usually a Bernese mountain dog or a mastiff in my spot on the bed.

One day in the spring of 2004 I received an e-mail from a woman named Pat Fish. She told me that she had read one of my books and really liked it, but the main reason she was writing was to praise my work in dog rescue.

She described herself as a volunteer for a golden retriever rescue group, and went on to say that she was currently fostering a three-year-old golden that would never find a home. It seemed that he had grand mal seizures, and the clusters were so intense that it was unlikely anyone would take on the responsibility and expense of bringing him into their home. She attached a picture of a beautiful golden retriever, who she said was named Bumper.

Seizures in dogs, as in humans, can be very violent and frightening to watch. But they are rarely dangerous; there is no concern that the dog might swallow its tongue, and they usually run their course in a few minutes. Afterward, the dog might be disoriented for a short while, but he or she soon snaps out of it. The only real danger, as I understand it, is that the dog's body temperature can get dangerously high if the seizure goes on for too long.

There is also no psychological component to epileptic seizures for canines; when it's over, it's over. Add to that the fact that drugs often control the problem quite well and it really is not that big a deal, as long as you know what to expect.

But in our experience, epilepsy is a major deterrent to prospective owners. And with seizures as frequent and violent as those Pat described in Bumper, I could imagine that placement would be extraordinarily difficult.

I was leaving the house right after I received the e-mail; I was picking Debbie up at her office and taking her to the airport. So I replied to Pat, giving her my cell number and asking her to call me.

She called a few minutes later, and I asked her where she lived. My thought was that if it was somewhere in or near

California, we would offer to take Bumper into our home. We already had three epileptic dogs in the house; a fourth would not be a hardship. So long as he was not dog aggressive, we'd love to have him.

She said that she lived in Louisville, so I quickly told her I'd get back to her in five minutes. I picked up Debbie, who was preparing to fly to Louisville on the Taco Bell corporate jet. Taco Bell's parent company, Yum! Brands, is based there. She told me what I knew she would: that if the rescue group could get Bumper ready, she would pull whatever strings necessary to enable Bumper to fly back to us the next day on the Taco Bell corporate jet.

I called Pat back and told her the news. She seemed excited at the prospect of it, and told me that she would immediately contact the powers that be within the rescue group and get back to me.

She did contact me later that night, but with bad news. She said that she just couldn't get it organized in time, implying that the leaders of the group weren't prepared to make that quick a decision. She was obviously disappointed that it wasn't going to work out, but she was just a volunteer with the group and did not have the authority to make that kind of call.

It made sense to me. Rescue people take very seriously the well-being of dogs in their protection. To send this one to live with some lunatic stranger who already had thirty dogs in his house is something that I would not have done if I had been in their position.

There was no reason to press her on it, since she had little say in the matter. And it wasn't a tragedy to us; we would have welcomed Bumper, but it's not like he was now going to die in a shelter. I knew that Pat would take good care of him, so I wished her well, and I told Debbie that there would be no shedding on the corporate jet.

Three weeks later, as I was preparing to go on tour for my third book, *Bury the Lead,* Pat called back. She told me that the rescue group had done an about-face and now really wanted to make this adoption happen. I suspect they had done some research on us and determined that we would be an acceptable home for Bumper.

However, they were loath to fly Bumper out to us, since in his condition they didn't deem it safe for him to fly in the bottom of a commercial plane.

Albuquerque was going to be my last stop on the tour, and Pat said that she and her husband, Dick, would be willing to drive Bumper from Louisville to Albuquerque. It would be a very long trip for them, but the effort was typical of the kind of people I later found them to be. I told her that if they drove Bumper there, I'd cancel my flight, rent a car, and drive him back to California.

So they showed up at the bookstore signing with Bumper. I was glad they did for a couple of reasons, including the fact that had they not shown up, I would have been the only person at the signing. I would have had to sign a book to myself, maybe with the inscription, "To David, an extraordinary author and friend and a damned good-looking guy."

Did Hemingway and Faulkner have to put up with such indignities?

The store was actually in the process of going out of business; half the shelves were empty, and boxes were everywhere. So Pat, Dick, and I spent the time talking about and petting Bumper, who was every bit as beautiful as his picture had shown him to be. And, Pat was pleased to report, perfectly house-trained.

We eventually said our good-byes, and Bumper and I set out in the rental car for Southern California. We didn't hit any traffic leaving, because did I mention that not a single person showed up for the signing?

It's a twelve-hour ride, so we started it by stopping at McDonald's and getting Bumper a double hamburger. Then we drove for four hours and checked into a hotel for the night. Once we got our room, I took him outside for a walk. House-trained as he was, he hadn't gone in a long while and must have been holding it in.

We walked for forty-five minutes, but he wasn't inclined to do anything, so I took him back to the room. I figured that if I woke up during the night, I'd take him out for another chance.

It turned out that Bumper was house-trained; he just wasn't hotel-trained. As soon as we got to the room, literally as soon as I closed the door, he pissed all over it. I yelled at him, but if he was intimidated or remorseful, he hid it very well. He smiled at me the whole time.

Today Bumper is twelve years old, and one of the best dogs we've ever had. For a while he had some difficult times with seizures, but he had his last one five years ago and hasn't looked back. He's slowing down but is in remarkably good shape, and I have grudgingly forgiven him for pissing in the hotel.

Bumper, I am happy to report, was one of the twenty-five on the trip to Maine. And fortunately, he is RV-trained.

Willie Boy

People have all kinds of reasons for giving up their pets. Some of them are justified, but the majority of them are stupid and uncaring. They also have all kinds of ways to do it, and one of the more annoying ones is when they board their dog somewhere, give a fake name, and never return to get it.

One day Debbie and I were approached by the receptionist at Bay Cities Veterinary Hospital, our vet in Marina del Rey, looking for a favor. People had dropped off for boarding their fourteen-year-old chow mix, Willie, and subsequently vanished. Willie had by then been stuck in a cage for four weeks, and they had no idea what to do with him.

Since our foundation was based at that vet, they wondered if we could somehow place Willie in a home. We said that we would try, but the likelihood of placing a fourteen-year-old chow mix is virtually nonexistent.

The headline Debbie wrote for Willie's ad in the *Los Ange-*

les Times was "Tell Them Willie Boy Is Here," and the copy went on to honestly and accurately explain the difficult circumstances that Willie found himself in.

The afternoon that the ad ran, I got a phone call from a man who simply said, "I'm interested in Willie." The voice was simultaneously powerful and very familiar, but I couldn't place it.

As with all prospective adopters, I asked the man a series of questions, mostly about why he was interested in Willie, what kind of home he had, whether he had other dogs, whether Willie would be an inside dog, that kind of thing.

He explained that he'd had two dogs, but one had recently died. The remaining dog was a female twelve-year-old chow mix, and it just seemed that Willie would likely make a good companion for her.

His answers were all perfect; there was little doubt that he would pass our screening process. The prospect for success improved even more when I asked him his name, and he said, "Chuck Heston."

I was talking to Charlton Heston, and he wanted "Willie Boy."

Now, it should be pointed out that Mr. Heston and I were on opposite ends of the political spectrum, and I was never really a big fan of most of his movies. Even though I'm a fanatic Giants fan, I probably prefer Ben Roethlisberger to Ben-Hur.

But Willie, as far as I could tell, was apolitical, and not much of a movie buff. And he and I agreed that anyone who would go out of his way to provide a home for an abandoned senior chow mix had a lot going for him. Besides, Willie was about to live out his life sucking down designer biscuits, so he was adamant that I not screw this up.

I had met Mr. Heston once, early in my movie marketing

career. It was on a movie called *Soylent Green,* and our encounter was brief. That was nearly forty years ago, and the details are vague in my mind; it was probably in a meeting or maybe at a screening. Certainly he would never remember me.

In any event, we were not going to have a chance to get reacquainted. He sent an assistant to pick up Willie, a very nice lady who gave me all the proper assurances that he would be well taken care of. Willie drove off from the vet's office as if he were the king of England.

The woman also brought with her a check for $2,500 from Mr. Heston as a donation to our foundation, and similar donations were made for each of the next three years.

I'm not sure how long Willie Boy lived, but I'm pretty sure of one thing: the old guy went out in style.

"Do You Take Pets?"

I bought a book on pet-friendly travel, which included a lengthy list of U.S. hotels and motels that accepted pets. I set out to learn what our options were, even though it was way too early to make any reservations. Not only did we not yet know how we would travel, but we also didn't know our route. To complete the trifecta, even if we did decide on a route, we hadn't yet figured out how far we could travel each day, so we wouldn't know where to plan to stop.

To say we were at square one would be to give us way too much credit.

So at that point I was just trying to gauge how hotels would react to our request. I decided to be honest, not because that's my natural instinct or because I thought there was any kind of moral imperative in play here.

Rather, my fear was that if I lied, we'd show up at a hotel and of course be unable to sneak the dogs in undetected, and we'd get turned away. And the only way we wouldn't be detected was if the proprietor was in a coma. A very deep, kept-alive-by-machines coma.

So the first place I called was a motel outside of Salt Lake City. A woman cheerily told me that they were very dog-friendly, even providing water dishes and biscuits. Of course, a refundable cleaning deposit was required; fifty dollars for a dog under thirty pounds, and seventy-five dollars for one larger than that.

I hadn't done the math, but I was pretty sure that we would be traveling with well over a ton of dog, so the cleaning deposit would probably be the GDP of a third-world country.

I told her the whole story, not because I wanted to stay in that hotel, but more to get her reaction and advice. She thought it was pretty much the funniest thing she had ever heard, but when she stopped laughing, she admitted that there was no way her manager would ever agree to it.

She wouldn't even have the nerve to ask him, and she doubted there was a hotel manager on the planet who would go for it. Other than that, she was really encouraging.

So at that point, three months before the trip, we had no way to travel, not enough people to travel with, and no places to stay or eat along the way.

Things were really cooking.

Emmit Luther and his wife, Deb, own a bunch of Taco Bells in Georgia and live on a farm outside Atlanta. Emmit is something of a character: a big, burly, very funny guy who would happily give you the shirt off his back, though it would almost always be an SEC football jersey.

We knew the Luthers through Debbie's job at Taco Bell, and we had spent time with them at football games and had vacationed with them once. We considered them good friends, and when they heard about our predicament, they demonstrated that we were right to make that judgment.

Deb would have to be in the office, but Emmit wanted to go on the trip. I should just let him know when to be in California, and he was in.

Not only was he in, but he was perfect. He told me that when he was younger, he drove an eighteen-wheeler cross-country for a living. Because I'm an analytical guy, I figured that an eighteen-wheeler must be a vehicle with eighteen wheels. If we wound up using vehicles of some sort, I doubted they'd have more wheels than that, so it would likely be a piece of cake for Emmit.

He was also an animal lover, and on the lunacy scale lived a life that ranked right up there with Debbie's and mine. He and Deb had a house- and farmful of various animals, including many dogs and goats.

Emmit would fit in on the trip very, very well.

One of my favorite places to do book signings is Houston. I generally do them as a benefit for Golden Beginnings rescue group, in conjunction with a terrific mystery bookstore called Murder By The Book.

As rescue groups go, Golden Beginnings is as good as there is. We've actually gotten two goldens from them, very old dogs that were hard to place. One was a sweet, smallish dog named Buddy, and the other was a one-eared dog they called Van Gogh. They were fantastic dogs, and though neither lived very long after we got them, we were lucky to have them in our home.

I had gotten friendly with two of the women in the group, Joanie Patrick and Robin Miller, and I invited them to dinner the night before the signing. Robin brought along her husband, Randy, whom I had not previously met.

The conversation got around to our trip to Maine, which was no surprise, since every conversation I had with everyone was about that. When Randy heard about it, he didn't hesitate; he wanted to be a part of the trip.

Randy would bring a great deal to the party. He and Robin were dedicated rescue people who had a special soft spot for senior and special-needs dogs. As a retired airline executive with an expertise in airline overhaul and maintenance, he knew how to fix stuff. That would perfectly complement me, since I knew how to break stuff. Like Emmit, Randy also had considerable cross-country driving experience.

I learned later that Randy has a real protective instinct. He felt his presence and expertise could actually help ensure the safety of everyone on the trip, human and dog, and that alone was enough to get him to sign on.

The bonus part of this was that both Emmit and Randy were "real" men. They even had toolsheds at home. Until that point, our group had consisted of Cyndi, Debbie, and me, which meant we were suffering from a "real man" deficit.

But all of a sudden we had two. And if you included me, we still had two.

Among the things we didn't have was a date for the trip to begin. We had bought a house in Maine that was lived in only during the summers, and we were both renovating and winterizing it. A number of construction issues were coming up, and the target date kept getting pushed back.

May became June, and June became July. I told our contractors that we weren't in a huge hurry, but that once we set on a date, then that had to be the date. Once we put the trip into motion, there was no reset button to press.

Of course, while we weren't rushing them, the move had to be accomplished no later than October. We couldn't take a chance on hitting a snowstorm on the way; we might never be heard from again.

They finally had a date that they were comfortable with . . . September 10. We told Cyndi, Randy, and Emmit, and they were fine with it. Cyndi had a friend, Mary Lynn Dundas, who wanted to go along as well, so with Debbie and me, we had six people. No way that would be enough, but we were making progress.

Hunter / Tudor—Tudor/Hunter

When one of my books is released, I usually go on a signing tour of varying length. Many of the scheduled events are set up by bookstores or libraries in combination with local rescue groups.

It's a win-win for me. The fact that rescue groups are involved increases the attendance considerably, and I therefore sign and sell more books. Even more significant, they are able to raise money for rescue by selling tickets, having auctions and raffles, and things like that.

Even when it's not a rescue event per se, smart bookstore owners alert the local rescue groups that I'm coming, and they show up to hear a fellow dog lunatic speak.

Very often they bring dogs to the signings, sometimes with the store owners' permission, sometimes without. I'm always pleased by dog visits, because after some time on the road, I generally need a dog fix. The face of a golden retriever feels like home.

One of the best mystery bookstores in the country is the Poisoned Pen, in Scottsdale, Arizona. The owner, Barbara Peters, has a well-deserved reputation as a savvy, dedicated, and respected bookseller. She has a forceful personality, and my reaction when she tells me to come to the store for a signing is to stand up, look her in the eye, and say, "Yes, Barbara."

Barbara never fails to alert the local golden retriever rescue group that I'm going to be there, and they usually get into the spirit by bringing a golden with them. A few years ago, when *Dog Tags* came out, they brought two of them to a Sunday-afternoon signing.

The dogs were nothing short of spectacular. They were twelve-year-old brothers, and if there is such a thing as identical twins in dogs, they would have been it. They had spent their entire lives together but were now homeless and under the care of the rescue group. They had been prettied up for the occasion with bandanas that said, respectively, "Hunter" and "Tudor."

Older dogs are always very difficult to place, and in this case it was even tougher, because the rescue group understandably had no intention of splitting up two dogs that had been together for twelve years. Therefore, they had to find a potential adopter willing to take two senior dogs.

Good luck with that.

So the group had come up with the brilliant idea that I should take them, which was more than fine with me. I didn't even bother to call Debbie, since she would have been disappointed that there were only two of them.

It was summer, and therefore way too hot to consider putting them in the bottom of an airplane. I canceled my flight, rented a car, and drove the six hours home. Since Bumper had liked it so much, we stopped at a McDonald's for a welcome-to-the-family treat, and off we went.

When we got home it was time to introduce them to their thirty-one brothers and sisters. We generally do this outside, in a fenced-in area. It's usually one dog we're introducing, and the group descends on the newcomer to check him or her out. It can be intimidating for the new arrivals, but after fifteen minutes or so, they're used to it and starting to feel at home.

This time was different; we were introducing two new dogs, and the reaction was hilarious. Our dogs didn't know where to go first, and they bounced from one to the other like pinballs. It served to cut in half the stress that Hunter and Tudor went through, since they each had only half the energy directed at them.

The only problem was that our dogs feel empowered to set the fashion trends in our house; for instance, they have decreed that all human clothing be covered with dog hair.

In this case they quickly decided that they weren't fond of the bandana look. So within minutes, they tore the offending garments off Hunter and Tudor, leaving them bandana-less.

That wouldn't ordinarily be a big deal, except for the fact that it also left them nameless. Once the bandanas with their names were removed, we had absolutely no way to know which was which, since they looked exactly alike. Our solution, which we employed for all the time that we had them, was to call each of them "Hunter-Tudor."

They didn't seem to mind.

Interestingly, Hunter and Tudor had pretty much nothing to do with each other once they lived with us. Each of our dogs usually has a base of operations where they feel comfortable hanging out and sleeping. In the case of Hunter and Tudor, one of them spent almost all his time in our bedroom, and the other in my office.

It's not that they weren't dog friendly; they interacted frequently and pleasantly with their new housemates. They just showed no interest in each other.

We had Hunter/Tudor and Tudor/Hunter for three years, which means they were fifteen when they died. That's a long life for a golden, though clearly not long enough.

They died within three days of each other. I don't mention that to imply that one died of a broken heart from losing his brother. Because of where they hung out in the house, I can't even be sure that he knew his brother was gone. But there is certainly that possibility, and if I've learned one thing, it is that the heart of a dog is more than large enough to be broken.

"Poop" . . . Just This Once

I don't like the word "poop," and I can't say it without feeling ridiculous. It doesn't sound serious enough and seems way too delicate. The stuff that I seem to spend my entire life cleaning up is . . . drumroll, please . . . dog shit.

I've had four back surgeries, and I would estimate that dog shit is responsible for four of my back surgeries. So while I'm sure no one is particularly crazy about it, I probably like it even less than most.

In California, where the weather is always annoyingly fine, we had double doors that led out to our property, which was fenced in. The doors were always open, so the dogs could go in and out easily. We never considered a "doggie door," since ours would have had to be huge.

Of course, that did cause other problems. In the summer, the open doors let air-conditioning out and bugs in. In the winter, on a cold night, you could hang meat in our house.

So I came up with a solution, the only successful handyman-type idea I've ever had. We hung strips of clear plastic from the top of the open doors to the bottom, sort of like you would see in a car wash. The dogs could go in and out through the strips, which would then fall back into place. It certainly wasn't perfect or airtight, but for someone who can't change a light-bulb, it was inspired brilliance.

But the dog shit would accumulate outside, and the area required frequent maintenance. I was adept at using a dustpan and broom; Debbie is a maestro with a plastic bag. Once the shit is picked up, we hose down the entire area. It's not fun, but not doing it is even less desirable.

Moving to Maine presented us with a bigger problem. It gets cold there, and snowy and muddy. If we used the open-door "car wash" approach, we would freeze to death.

Our contractor decided the solution was to build an extra room onto the house. The dogs would walk into that room through a doggie door, and then out through another one to the yard. The room would be the buffer, helping to keep out the cold from the main house, and bearing the brunt of the snow and mud as it was tracked in.

Maybe I'm old-fashioned, but I didn't want to have to build a "shit room." It would have been ridiculously expensive, would have looked silly, and seemed wholly unnecessary.

So we tasked the contractor with finding or building a doggie door that would solve our problem. It had to be big enough for Wanda the mastiff to get through, which is to say we needed something roughly the size of the Lincoln Tunnel.

And they did it. If you ever find yourself in Maine, needing an enormous doggie door, just call Hervochon Construction.

They rose to the occasion, on this and every other bizarre request we made.

Wanda has to duck only a little bit to go through the clear plastic, which immediately snaps back into place, with the benefit of magnets. It's a remarkable feat of engineering.

Unfortunately, the stuff still has to be cleaned up. I've abandoned my dustpan and broom for a snow shovel, which I use year-round. But the job gets quite complicated in the winter, when the area is covered with snow and ice.

Not to get too technical for laypeople not involved in the shit removal business who might be reading this, but it's a simple principle of physics. Shit stuck in ice tends to remain in ice until it melts. Before it melts, it's impossible to remove. After it melts, I don't want to get close enough to remove it.

It's a dilemma.

Also, when it gets to the hosing-down-the-area part, which is essential to the process, the hose gets frozen in the winter, as do my face and hands.

Suffice it to say that it's still a work in progress, but we unfortunately get a chance to practice our technique every winter's day.

Solving the "How"

After very careful consideration and a few dozen calls made by Cyndi Flores and me, it seemed as if RVs were the only possible solution, if we could somehow acquire them. They would provide relative comfort for both dogs and humans, would hold a good number of both, and could be slept in. Based on our online research about the size, it seemed like we would need three of them to be comfortable.

Buying three RVs was clearly cost-prohibitive, and a company would have had to be as insane as we are to rent us any. Anyone who has ever been in our house knows that once this many dogs enter the picture, any picture, nothing is ever the same again.

So I would have to lie. It would be a lie I could get away with, since the company would have no way of knowing about it. It wasn't as if they'd be with us on the trip. I knew we'd be ultimately responsible for any damage caused, and would certainly have to clean the vehicles thoroughly before returning them. So in that sense it would be a relatively harmless lie.

We simply had no other choice.

I called the largest RV rental company, Cruise America, and inquired about prices and availability. I wasn't planning to tell them how many dogs would be onboard, but I wanted to make sure that at least one or more were allowed. We'd clean up as best we could after the trip, but it wouldn't be perfect, and it would be hard to claim that humans did the shedding.

So a few minutes into the conversation I asked, as nonchalantly as I could, "What's your policy toward pets?"

"We allow them," the woman said.

"Does it matter how many? We're trying to decide whether to bring our dogs, and we have three of them." I had clearly checked my dignity at the door.

"Doesn't matter at all," she said. "As long as you return the vehicle in the same condition as you received it."

There it was. With those few words, she made her decision for us. If the future Jeopardy! *answer is "The maniacs took them to Maine," then the question will be "What are RVs?"*

Of course, like everything else, the answer wasn't as simple as it seemed. For example, they wouldn't rent them one way, so we were going to have to drive them back to California, albeit dogless. And there were all kinds of operational issues, like water and propane and toilet flushing, that in a million years I wouldn't know how to handle. But with Emmit and Randy on board, those "real man" issues would be manageable.

Debbie and I went to the local place where we would pick up the vehicles, to judge what size we'd need. They seemed close to ideal; there was even a sleeping area above the front seat that the dogs wouldn't be able to get to. Sleeping with our group of dogs is an acquired taste, and this way the other humans on the trip would not have to learn it on the fly.

The vehicles came in three sizes, and we actually walked around the inside of them, figuring out where dogs could sleep, so as to judge what our needs were. We finally rented two of the largest and one medium. With twenty-five dogs, the most one would have to accommodate would be nine, and that seemed very feasible. In fact, it would likely be more comfortable than our house.

The RVs also had a bathroom with a shower, as well as a kitchen with a refrigerator, a stove, and a microwave. We would be totally self-sufficient and wouldn't have to rely on hotels and restaurants, which was a major relief.

I called Cruise America a few more times to try and cajole them into letting us return the vehicles in Maine or Boston, rather than drive them all the way back to California. They couldn't do that, explaining that the RVs had to be in certain places for the next renters.

But they came up with a way that we could return them to Manassas, Virginia, which was a hell of a lot better than California. Cyndi Flores offered to drive one back, since she now lived in Virginia. Obviously, we still had to make arrangements for the other two.

In terms of transportation, we were set, and if John Travolta finally called, I could tell him to keep his damn plane.

Now all we needed were some more humans.

Weasel

Debbie and I were in the SEACCA shelter in Downey; we had limited open rescue space at that moment, and had room for only three more dogs. Debbie saw a smallish one, about a year and a half old, black, white, and gray, that looked unlike any we had ever seen.

But that's not what caught her eye. What was most noticeable about this dog was how scared she was. She was in a cage with four other dogs, and she looked panicked to be there. When we went over to the cage, she pulled away from us; she was afraid of humans as well.

We didn't take her with us, but it haunted Debbie for the next few days. So she went back, knowing that the dog would not have been adopted but fearing that she might have already been put down.

She was still there, petrified but alive, and Debbie rescued her. We took her to our vet for a checkup and a bath, and I was there when she arrived. She was adorable, and we named her Ellie, but we knew that Ellie wouldn't be adopted anytime soon. She was just too frightened and would never go near a potential adopter.

So over the next month, we worked with her. We petted her, took her for walks, and tried to socialize her as much as possible. We hired a trainer, and we asked her to make Ellie a priority. And it was working; she gradually started coming out of her shell, at least with us. But with other people, not so much.

Finally a woman came by and fell in love with her; in fact, she also fell in love with a dog named Clark. Clark was ten years old, and therefore mellow, but Ellie was not high-energy either. The adopter was a senior citizen herself, and we had some concerns when she told us she wanted to adopt both Clark and Ellie. But she convinced us she could handle it, and she was obviously a dog lover who would care for them well, so we let her do so.

The phone call came about three hours later. The woman, who lived in Culver City, had taken Ellie and Clark for a walk. When they got back inside her house, she dropped the leashes, not realizing that she had not completely closed the door behind her.

Ellie was out of there.

I drove around Culver City for three days looking for her. I can't stand thinking that any dog is out there in the world alone, but in Ellie's case it was even more troubling. I figured she must have been scared to death.

I didn't have any luck, but then I got a call from the West LA shelter. Whenever we placed a dog, Debbie put one of our tags on them before they left the vet's office. It was for situations just like this. So the shelter person, who knew us quite well, saw our tag and called.

I was hopeful it was Ellie, but it didn't have to be, so I asked the guy what she looked like.

He laughed and said, "I'm not sure. Sort of like a weasel."

I went to the shelter, and it was definitely her. Not only did she have our tag on, but she was still dragging the woman's leash. So we rescued her from a shelter for the second time.

The woman had decided she couldn't handle two dogs and didn't want Ellie back. That was fine with us, since we wouldn't have let her have her anyway. She was happy with Clark, and we felt that one dog was all she needed.

Debbie felt like Ellie had been through too much to put her back in a cage, so we brought her home. It was a violation of our "only old or sick dog" pledge, but even back then, the pledge was not exactly an ironclad rule.

We decided that the name Ellie hadn't worked that well for her to that point, so we changed it. From then on she was Weasel.

The day I brought Weasel home, Debbie was sick in bed. I put Weasel on the bed with her, but she was scared, and she proceeded to piss all over it.

Not an auspicious debut.

As all the dogs did, Weasel soon found a place where she was comfortable; in her case, it was under our bed. She stayed there all day every day, venturing out only to eat and go outside to the bathroom. Amazingly, despite the pissing-on-the-bed fiasco, she was house-trained.

Gradually, over a period of months, she grew to trust us, and she would come out for long periods and hang out with us and the other dogs. But that's where the trust ended. If we had a visitor in the house, you couldn't pry her out from under the bed with a crowbar.

There were no exceptions, and no time limits to this. My father came to stay with us for a week from his home in Florida. He hadn't visited in a few years, so he'd never seen me up close as a dog maniac. He could not believe what our house was like, and he didn't get to see all the dogs; he never once saw Weasel. She had lived with us for two years by that point, but while there was a stranger in the house, she stayed under the bed.

When visitors weren't around, she would go out on our property and display her eccentricities. She would climb trees; I swear that's true. And she'd bring things back and leave them on our living room floor. One day it was a deflated football. Another day it was a dead lizard.

I preferred the football.

Weasel lived in our Santa Monica house for five years. When we moved our thirty-seven dogs to Orange County, the arrival of the movers sent her scurrying for cover under the bed. I will never forget the look on her face when they took the mattress and bed frame, leaving her exposed.

When we left Orange County for Maine, eleven years after that, Weasel was the only one of the thirty-seven Santa Monica dogs still alive. Debbie and I had been hoping that she would make it to Maine, and she did.

Weasel died four months after we arrived in Maine, at the grand old age of seventeen. I think she held on as long as she did because she knew how much we wanted her to.

Saying good-bye to any one of our dogs is hard, but in Weasel's case it was that much harder. She was the only dog we had that had spanned the years with us. She was there almost from the time we started in rescue, and she stayed with us until we completed our journey.

I know for a fact that she spent almost sixteen of her seventeen years loved and doted on. Yet in her mind it never totally made up for the one year that had left her so wary and frightened.

But she trusted us, totally and completely, and that was the greatest gift she could have given us.

Weasel was a keeper.

Louis

I was contacted by the Pasadena animal shelter, which is about as good a shelter as you will find in Southern California. They had two goldens, which we would later name Louis and Gus, that had been found stray together. They properly would only place them both in the same home, and had done so, but the dogs had been returned.

I was surprised that the shelter needed us, since they have a very good adoption rate. We had been called on by them only once before, to rescue a twelve-year-old epileptic golden named Yogi.

Once I got there, the reason they'd called became obvious. Both dogs were beautiful, but while Louis was three years old, Gus was eleven. More significant, Gus had terrible separation anxiety. When the people who adopted them from Pasadena left them alone in the house, Gus had broken through a window to get out. The cuts on his face testified to the truth of the story.

We got them home, and any separation anxiety disappeared. With all the other dogs around, there is no such thing as separation. Both dogs were fabulous, and we were thrilled to have them.

Two days into their stay with us, the woman from the shelter called to say that a mistake had been made, and that Louis actually was wanted by the director of the shelter to be his family pet. The good news, she told us, was that we could keep Gus. In other words, they wouldn't ordinarily split Louis and Gus up, but since it was the director who wanted Louis, they'd make an exception in this case.

I briefly tried to picture Debbie's reaction if I agreed to this. It's too graphic to go into, but it's fair to say that I would have been living in a shelter myself within the hour. But I was actually smart enough to figure this one out on my own even without the fear of Debbie to coerce me. I told the woman exactly what I thought of her plan, and what she could tell the director.

Louis was staying.

It was right up there with the finest moves I've ever made. The best way I can describe Louis is to say that Debbie considers him Tara's direct descendant, and trust me, no higher praise can be offered.

He is perfect in every respect, so much so that he has never barked.

Not once. Ever.

We could use a lot more like Louis.

Sally and Jack

Whenever a story comes on the news involving anything approaching animal cruelty, both Debbie and I rush to turn the television off. It's not the most mature approach; it just bothers us to see animals in distress when we can't do anything about it.

Just such a story was highly publicized in Southern California a few years back, and it was awful. A woman living in the Mojave Desert had 250 animals on her property, 90 percent of which were dogs. They went uncared for and undernourished, living in horribly filthy conditions. The woman was arrested and convicted on multiple felony counts, which was the trigger that allowed rescue groups to go in.

I got a call from a member of one of those groups; she told me that there were two purebred goldens among the dogs and asked if we would take them. I obviously agreed, and I drove to LA to meet the woman and the dogs, which she had just extricated from the scene.

They weren't remotely close to golden retrievers, though both had a small amount of gold in their coat. Sally is a small-ish short-haired shepherd mix, and my best guess is that Jack has shepherd and Brittany spaniel in him.

Sally had permanent cut marks on her face, probably the result of fighting for the little available food, and an ear hematoma that needed immediate surgery. Jack was emaciated— with his mellow disposition, he probably never even entered the food fights.

Both are beyond sweet, and probably like petting as much as any two dogs we've ever had. We have a chaise up in our bedroom in Maine that Sally has appropriated as her own. Jack sits on a chair in my office, and as I walk by he leans his head down slightly, so as to be in the "petting-receiving" position.

I hope the other Mojave dogs are doing close to as well as these two.

They are what animal rescue is all about.

The Team Comes Together

We had six people signed on: Debbie and me, Cyndi Flores, Mary Lynn Dundas, Emmit Luther, and Randy Miller. Of those, Mary Lynn had said she would not be comfortable driving a vehicle that large. That was understandable; I wasn't looking forward to it myself.

But it meant that we had only five drivers. Unless Wanda and a few of the goldens could take shifts behind the wheel, we were way short.

And then the human floodgates opened.

I used to do book signings at a store called Mysteries to Die For, in Thousand Oaks, California. It was a great store that has recently and unfortunately had to close, a victim of declining sales at independent bookstores around the country.

Terri Nigro is a woman who came to a number of the signings, and she had e-mailed me saying she enjoyed the talks and liked the books. But because she was there, she had to hear my incessant, increasingly pathetic pleas for ideas about how to make the trip.

She wrote to say that however we were going to do it, she and her husband, Joe, would like to join us on the trip. I didn't remember meeting her at the signings and wasn't sure who she was. Since I was only "talking" to her via e-mail, there was always the chance that she and her husband were ax murderers.

Of course, it's not that being ax murderers would have disqualified them in my eyes. We desperately needed help in the form of volunteers, and as long as they'd be willing to leave their axes at home, we'd welcome them with open paws.

Terri told me that she owned a word-processing business, and also worked at a nonprofit satellite TV ad agency. More significant, she said that Joe owned an upholstery repair business, specializing in restaurants. What this meant was that Joe seemed like a good candidate to join Emmit and Randy in the "real man" section of the team. With three RVs, this would mean we'd have one real man for each vehicle.

So Terri and Joe were in, and they even offered to drive one of the RVs back to Virginia at the end. I was thrilled, but a little wary. Could there really be people this nice?

With Terri and Joe's signing up, we had eight people, which included seven drivers. That might be enough to make it, but not comfortably. We definitely needed more, but we had no idea where to find them. Crazy people don't grow on trees.

Just two days later, Debbie was describing the situation to a friend of hers, Cindy Spodek Dickey, who lived in Seattle. She was one of the only people we had ever had over for dinner at our house in Orange County, a couple of years earlier. It was an evening that stamped her as both a dog lover and totally fearless.

When someone enters our house, we instruct them not to pet or even acknowledge the dogs until they have calmed down. Best to ignore them, as difficult as that is while being mobbed. Petting only excites them and increases the energy and decibel level, if such a thing is possible.

Cindy had disregarded our instructions and launched into full-scale two-handed petting as soon as she entered. She even bent down to do so.

It wasn't pretty; at one point I actually lost complete sight of her in the canine mosh pit. I was trying to figure out how I would explain the disaster to the police when she stood up, relatively unscathed, laughing.

This was a woman to be reckoned with.

Cindy apparently hadn't gotten any saner since that evening. As Debbie was telling her about the trip, I could hear her screaming through the phone from the other room. She absolutely wanted in, and she couldn't believe Debbie hadn't asked her. She vowed that whenever we did it, however we did it, she was going to be a part of it.

That made nine.

Erik Kreider designs my Web site, a job that is as completely unsatisfying as any could be. I pay almost no attention to it and provide very little information for him to work with. He does a really good job of it, but he could do much better if I put in the effort.

Erik heard about the trip when I solicited his help to get online suggestions for how we should do it. He immediately realized that we were going to have to drive, and he volunteered to come along.

Actually, he pretty much insisted, though I wasn't particularly resistant. He told me that he drives long distances quite often and loves doing it, especially the night-driving part. That made him *absolutely perfect for us, since I really enjoy night sleeping. Best of all, he offered to drive the third RV back to Virginia, taking me off the hook.*

A side benefit, though none was needed, was that Erik is a very funny guy, and a terrific writer in his own right. His presence and commentary would brighten the trip, and in my eyes, it was a trip that needed considerable brightening.

Erik wanted to bring his son, Nick, along. Nick is around twenty years old, which made him too young to drive the vehicles, since the rental company required that drivers be at least twenty-five. But he could help in other ways, and there would be plenty of other ways.

I figured it was kind of a father-son bonding thing, which was fine with me. I only wished that Erik had more kids.

The team seemed complete, but Cyndi Flores pointed out that we would need places to stop, mostly to walk the dogs, and they would have to be scouted out. You can't just let twenty-five dogs out along the highway; we would need confined areas, like dog parks. Of course, we didn't want to have to deal with the chaos involved with having our crew meet local dogs en route, so it was clear that planning would be required.

Cyndi took on the task of mapping out our route and contacting local rescue groups along the way. Our hope was that they could be there to help when we stopped, both in getting us to an appropriate area and in walking the dogs. We would even offer them the opportunity to get some publicity for our arrival, and possibly to use it for their fund-raising. Maybe they could charge five dollars a person to meet the traveling lunatics.

Cyndi started having some success, but I was worried about it. I worry about everything, but in this case it was justified.

We really had no idea how fast we'd be able to travel, for a myriad of reasons. Anything could happen, from a dog's getting sick and needing vet care to heavy traffic or a flat tire.

We might not make it in time to where local people were waiting, or we might get there earlier than planned. We didn't want to have to cut corners or drive more quickly and with less sleep simply because people were expecting us at a certain time. And we absolutely had no desire to have to sit in a town and hang around because we were ahead of schedule. The faster this trip was accomplished, the better.

Cyndi agreed, and said that she could enlist her daughter and a friend to drive a couple of hours ahead of our caravan, in one of our cars. They could scout out locations and tell us where to stop.

It seemed like a perfect solution, but then real life intervened and work prevented her daughter from coming along.

And then I came up with a great idea, my first and last of the trip.

We'd build our own dog parks.

Trapper

The Santa Monica shelter contacted us very rarely. It's a small place with an incredible adoption rate, and they were almost never in need of outside rescue help.

Enter Trapper, a beautiful two-year-old yellow Lab that had been taken in to the shelter badly injured, having reportedly been struck by a car.

He had a terrible wound on his leg, which the shelter vet saw as evidence that the car accident story was a fabrication. He had no doubt about what had really happened: Trapper had gotten his leg caught in a coyote trap, likely in the Santa Monica mountains.

The wound was clear around the leg, and bone could be seen from every direction. Additionally, there were bite marks just above it, as if the poor guy had tried to chew his leg off to escape the trap. It was horrible, and the shelter vet had real doubts that it would ever heal.

We took Trapper, and our vet shared those doubts. He operated, but even after the surgery was performed, there was no assurance that the leg could be saved.

Were I to call central casting and ask for the perfect dog adopters, they would send me Bruce and Kelly Green. A young couple living in Pasadena, they showed up one day looking for a yellow Lab. At the time, we didn't consider Trapper ready to be placed, but after talking to Bruce and Kelly, I decided they should see him.

To see Trapper was to fall in love with him, and they were certainly not immune to his charms. But they asked for time to think about it, since taking him home would represent a major commitment. Trapper was going to need ongoing and very difficult care for his injury.

They called the next day to say that they wanted him, even though I had told them it would be three weeks before he would be ready to go. Our vet, dissatisfied with Trapper's progress, was about to try a skin graft technique that he had never used before, in a desperate attempt to save the leg.

It worked, but ultimate healing would still take a very long time. Bruce and Kelly understood that, and when they got Trapper home, they were amazingly caring and attentive to his needs. Trapper bled frequently from the wound, though the vet said that this was good, because "only healthy cells bleed."

A turning point came when Kelly found a vinyl boot at a pet store that laced in the front and would stay on Trapper's leg. It allowed for healing to take place, and Trapper wound up wearing the boot for three months.

Today Bruce and Kelly describe Trapper as one of the great joys of their lives, and in fact the experience moved them to adopt and help many other special-needs dogs. And Trapper's boot hangs above their fireplace mantel.

Rescue can be an exhausting, draining "hobby," but it always seemed that when we felt we had reached the end of our rope, people like Bruce and Kelly Green would come along.

I wish there were more of them.

The Smell

We lived in a very nice neighborhood in Santa Monica, on Tenth Street between Montana and San Vicente Avenues. It was within easy walking distance of the shops and restaurants on Montana, the Third Street Promenade, and the beach.

All in all, it was a terrific place to live.

Unless you lived near us.

The homes were on very little land, with modest backyards and no more than fifteen feet between houses on either side. So, neighbors fifteen feet away, thirty or forty dogs . . . you do the math.

Our dogs were always house-trained, which in itself was remarkable. We rarely know the histories of the dogs we rescue, but certainly many must have been "outside dogs" before we got them. The law of averages says that it has to be the case, but there is also anecdotal evidence. Many times our dogs will have large calluses on their elbows, a sure sign that they've spent substantial time lying outside on hard, rough concrete.

If a dog was going to live outside, then there was no reason, and really no opportunity, to house-train it. Yet once these dogs came into our home, an interesting process took place. The other dogs would teach them to go outside; the newcomers would simply follow the group at bathroom time. I can't think of any other explanation for it.

But all those dogs doing their business in a backyard of maybe a thousand square feet presented some issues. It obviously had to be cleaned regularly, a task neither Debbie nor I relished, but which we did religiously. Unfortunately, urine cannot be swept up with a scooper.

So the place smelled.

And our neighbor complained.

We tried a number of things to deal with it. We sodded the area, but the urine quickly killed the grass. So we sodded it again, this time with better sod, and the urine killed it again.

If you're ever in a game of "sod, urine, scissors," you can be sure that urine beats sod.

Then, I forget why exactly, I had the bright idea to bring in sand and cover the backyard with it. So we did. We trucked in sand and turned the entire area into a beach; it was like watching a canine *Baywatch*. You haven't seen anything until you've seen a blind Saint Bernard frolicking on the beach.

It turned out to be an exquisitely stupid idea. The dogs hated it, probably because the sand was hot and annoying on their feet. They then tracked it into the house, destroying carpet and floor in a matter of days.

And it didn't stop the smell. Not even close.

Debbie was a tad critical of my sand idea, so I left it to her to come up with a different solution. And she did . . . borax. We removed the sand and then sprayed borax over the entire side of the yard near the neighbor's house. It was July, but it turned the place into what looked like a winter wonderland, as if pure snow was covering everything.

Within twenty-four hours the snow was 25 percent yellow, as the dogs got to work. And that percentage increased daily, so we spread more borax to cover it up. The borax got so deep that the dogs could barely walk in it, but, ever resourceful, they still managed to piss on it.

And still it smelled, so we decided to ditch the borax. Unfortunately, removing knee-deep borax is not the easiest thing in the world. There are no borax-plow operators in Santa Monica; it's not even that easy to find a snow shovel.

But we cleaned the stuff out, just in time to try our next trick. We got this perfumey, anti-smell stuff and sprayed it on the area at least five times a day. People driving by in their cars were gagging from the stench; it was like being trapped in a vat of cotton candy. Not surprisingly, the neighbor informed us that the new smell was far worse than the old one.

We had pretty much run out of ideas, and based on the quality of the ideas we had run out of, that wasn't necessarily a bad thing. So in a desperate measure, we constructed two parallel chain-link fences leading from the back of the house to the rear of the backyard.

This created a corridor about six feet wide for the dogs to use, a sort of bathroom bowling alley. It had the advantage of confining the origin of the offending odors to an area much farther from the neighbor, and it actually seemed to do the trick, at least as far as he was concerned.

It was just another example of life in the fast lane.

Because of our "open door" policy, flies were becoming particularly annoying, and Debbie came up with a way to deal with it. She bought a product called the Big Stinky, which was to be hung outside the room near the open door. It included a packet of some kind of solution, and to it we were supposed to add a quarter pound of raw fish.

This would apparently keep flies away, since flies are not idiots. Why would they want to be around the most disgusting thing in the history of the world?

Our experience with the Big Stinky lasted just one day. We never gave it a chance to see if it actually kept out the flies, because it's fair to say that there has never been a product more aptly named.

People often ask how we manage to keep the inside of our house clean. Of course I don't want to quibble, but that assumes that the inside of our house is clean. It isn't. In a perfect world, we try to minimize the level of dirty.

Hair is the biggest problem; it is everywhere. I recently took a laser printer in to be repaired, and when the guy opened the back, there was enough hair in it to make a coat.

It's a myth that dogs shed when the weather goes from cold to hot so that they'll be more comfortable in the summer. The truth is that they shed 365 days a year, twenty-four hours a day. I have no idea where all the hair comes from; maybe the groomer uses Rogaine on them. Otherwise they would be bald by now.

So we do the best we can. We go through vacuum cleaners at an amazing clip; in our garage in California we had six broken Orecks lined up against the wall, looking like a vacuum-cleaner version of the Rockettes. We also groom the dogs on a rotating basis, two or three a week, in an effort to cut down on the shedding.

Of course, hair is not the only problem; certain "incidents" take place with remarkable frequency, all with the capability of leaving stains. There are about 4 million products designed to clean up dog accidents, and trust me when I tell you that none of them works as advertised. Or maybe we just overwhelmed them.

One day Debbie and I were in bed watching television. There was a commercial for a dog cleaning product, and it showed a woman cleaning up after her boxer made a mess. At the end she's praising the product, and she holds it up and turns to the camera, a big smile on her face. "And I really need it," she says. "I have six of them."

Then the camera cuts to her dogs at her feet. The implication is clear: this woman is hilariously eccentric for having six dogs.

Of course, the camera didn't cut to the bed that Debbie and I were in, which we were sharing at the time with seven dogs. Add in the ones in the bedroom but not on the bed, and it totaled twenty-one.

If the lady in the commercial was nuts, what did that make us?

Totally nuts.

Harley and Dinah

Nancy Sarnoff of Perfect Pet Rescue, the friend that introduced us to dog rescue, would call periodically about dogs that
she had seen in the shelter but couldn't take herself. She spe-
cialized in small dogs, so when she fell in love with large ones,
we were her first call.

Harley and Dinah were two goldens that she saw in the
Downey animal shelter. Both had dirty and matted fur, and the
fact that they were nine years old meant they had little prospect
for adoption.

As expected, both fit into our house immediately. Harley
was completely friendly and easygoing, while Dinah was a
slightly heavier lift. She didn't like to be crowded by the other
dogs, and a dislike for being crowded is not a great quality to
have in our house. But she adapted, and there were no fights or
major disagreements.

People often ask me if I know the names of all our dogs.

Not only can I always name them, but I can do so quickly. The way I do it is by thinking room by room, since each has his or her own place to hang out.

Harley plants himself under my desk, and does so in Maine as he did in Orange County. Dinah, on the other hand, prefers the living room and a specific dog bed near the fireplace.

Two months before we moved to Maine, Dinah was diagnosed with an incurable cancer. The vet felt that she could have a good quality of life for six months, and he turned out to be right on target. Dinah died four months after our arrival in Maine. But she made it, and she will be missed.

Harley is fine, under my desk as I type this.

I Hate Home Depot

I hate Home Depot almost as much as I hate snakes, and even more than I hate the Dallas Cowboys and the New York Yankees. I hate it more than I hate broccoli and beets, and almost as much as I hate O. J. Simpson.

Home Depot stores are way too big and way too intimidating, and they make me feel totally inadequate. When I'm shopping for something, the employees can direct me to the right aisle, to the right shelf in that aisle, and to the right place on the shelf, and I still have no idea what I'm looking at.

Also, despite the fact that they have a large number of employees, there's always one too few when I get there. Every helpful employee is already talking to a customer, and every customer has a helpful employee to talk to. So I always park myself on the periphery of one of these conversations and wait for it to end.

Of course, I have no idea when that might be, because I can-

not understand anything they're saying. I recognize isolated words, like "rivets" or "caulking" or "voltage," but when put into the context of a Home Depot sentence, their meaning is completely obscured. It's like being in a foreign country, without any of the good vacation stuff.

Did I mention that I hate the place?

However, my pre-trip planning inevitably took me to the local Home Depot, to try to bring my big idea to fruition. I asked for the fencing department and was directed to an area about twelve miles from where I was standing. Walking from one end of that store to the other makes me feel like I'm going the wrong way on a people mover; I never seem to make progress getting there.

But when I finally arrived, I was shocked to find an employee walking through the department, and he stopped, smiled, and asked if I needed help.

I didn't know whether to talk to him or hug him.

I start every sentence I speak at Home Depot with the words "I have no idea what I'm talking about, but . . ." I say this even if I'm just asking where the restroom is. It places me in context, and insulates me from the subsequent and inevitable realization the salesperson would otherwise have that I have no idea what I'm talking about. My ignorance defines me, and I'm comfortable with that.

I told the guy that we were traveling cross-country with twenty-five dogs, waited for the surprise and laughter to run its course, and then told him what I was hoping to do. "I want fencing that we can put up and take down in a few minutes, and that will be strong enough that the dogs won't just run over it. We want to set up mini dog parks wherever we go."

"No problem," he said, as if he got requests like that every day.

He took me to an area that had rolled-up plastic fencing and rec-ommended two hundred feet of it. He also had stakes that could be placed into the fencing at whatever intervals we chose, and that could then be easily driven into the ground.

"So this can work?" I asked, since I'm not used to my ideas being feasible.

He shrugged. "Don't see why not. Is there anyone to stand around it and make sure the dogs don't try to crash it?"

I nodded. "We have eleven people."

He seemed surprised. "Friends of yours?"

"For now. That should last until Utah at the latest."

In order to reduce the chance that I would screw things up, I asked him to show me exactly how to set up the fence, including and especially how to put the stakes in the ground. Of course he made it look easy.

"You look like the kind of guy that would enjoy a trip like this," I said.

He laughed. "No chance."

"You sure? An opportunity to see the world . . . interact with wildlife . . . make new friends . . ."

He was not to be convinced, so I thanked him, loaded the fenc-ing into the car, and left. I felt like I had accomplished something physical, which is not a feeling I have very often. Maybe when I got home I could build a room onto the house or plow the lower thirty.

But the fact was that we were actually finally getting close to ready. We had the vehicles lined up, the people set and willing to go, and a plan, such as it was, in place.

Cyndi Flores was constantly evaluating what we were doing, and coming up with risk assessments on what could go wrong and how to cope with it if it did. Here's a chart she sent me, and when you read it, please keep in mind that this is a person I had never met.

Can you see why I named her Grand Exalted Empress of the Trip?

RISK ID	RISK NAME	DESCRIPTION
1	External issues cause travel delays	Weather, processing time at RV rental or various gas or dog stops, road conditions, traffic conditions create delays for one or more vehicles
2	Internal issues cause travel delays	Illness, accident with human or dog; human error; mechanical or non-mechanical issues with car or RV; dog gets loose on route and bolts or hides
3	Not enough well-rested drivers	Alternate drivers not able to get enough rest with ~10 dogs/2 humans in RV and having to try to sleep at non-regular hours
4	One RV becomes unavailable; no room for dogs	Vehicle (in this case RV) breaks down and is not repairable, or first day out we determine number of dogs and humans in RVs create an unsafe combination (i.e., human tripping over dog or dog getting splashed with something cooking on stove)
5	Actual RV drivers too few for driving straight through	Many people who have never driven RV before "discover" they aren't comfortable driving
6	RVs indescribably dirty after trip	Plastic proves difficult due to potential for slipping and covers prove inadequate to protect space over three days . . . it rains, there is mud and wet fur everywhere

RISK CONSEQUENCES	PROBABILITY OF OCCURRENCE RATE H/M/L	IMPACT RATE H/M/L	OVERALL RISK
Progress in route is delayed, potentially hours	H	M	
Progress on route is delayed, potentially hours; worst case could be day or having to leave someone behind on trip	M	H	
Triggers risk ID2 accident; creates unsafe condition for all	H	H	
Triggers risk ID2	L	H	
Triggers risk ID2	M	M	
Incur extra fees when returning RV vs. hiring help to clean RV vs. paying fee for late return and doing ourselves	H	L	

Crazy Sky and the Coyote

Wherever we live, we always make sure that we have a fence high enough and strong enough to keep the dogs from getting loose. They spend 99 percent of their time in the house, but if they were to see an animal outside the fence, they might try to go after it. We make sure that they can't.

At our home in Silverado, we had a decent-sized piece of property that was fenced in, and the dogs could roam wherever they wanted. Then there was a gated cement driveway, which the dogs were blocked from.

It worked quite well, and in the ten years we lived there, we had only one dog make it off the property. I'll talk about that later.

One day I got a call from a woman named Lorie Armbruster, a terrific lady who was a dedicated rescue person in Orange County. Her husband, Chris, worked with Debbie at Taco Bell. We occasionally took in dogs from her to live in our house, and obviously they were only the ones that her group could not otherwise place.

She was calling me with a special case. His name was Sky, and he was a magnificent three-year-old white shepherd, one of the most beautiful dogs I've ever seen.

Sky had something of a checkered past. He was owned by a family in a residential neighborhood, but he was a bit of a psycho, and he would go nuts whenever strangers approached the house. One time he got out of the house, ran wildly across the street toward a bunch of people, and in the process nipped a little girl.

There was no real damage, but the child was properly freaked out, and the neighbors decided that Sky was a menace. They demanded that the owners have him put down, but the owners loved Sky, and they wouldn't do it. Instead they gave Sky to the rescue group that Lorie represented, hoping that he would be placed in a good home in a neighborhood that he hadn't already terrorized.

But that wasn't good enough for the neighbors. They designated one of their crew to go to the rescue group, pretending to be a potential adopter of Sky. The plan was to adopt him and then have him put down. Fortunately, the rescue group somehow saw through the plan and held on to Sky, but they didn't then feel comfortable placing him in a normal home.

Which led Lorie to us, since we are anything but normal.

I met her at the place where Sky was being boarded, and I listened as she and another woman gave a very lengthy dissertation on Sky's rather delicate mental condition. He was unpredictable, had horrible separation anxiety, and had to be treated with kid gloves. They recommended that Sky not be left alone for at least a week, and then only for short periods, until we were sure that he would not go nuts.

I tried to explain to them that there is no such thing as separation anxiety in our house. When we leave, dogs are surrounded by a houseful of friends. We've had dogs that before we adopted them had gone through doors and windows when their owners left, but they displayed no such tendencies in our house. It's only humans that can be driven insane by being in our house; dogs find it perfectly appealing and comfortable.

Sky fit the pattern. He got to his new home and immediately became the perfect dog, mellow and unstressed. He got along great with the other dogs, and when we left he just laid on the couch and hung out. If we returned two hours later, he was still in his spot on the couch.

It was not atypical; dogs just behaved differently in our house than they did elsewhere. A number of trainers, at various times, had warned us that what we were doing could never work. They predicted fights and behaviors that we would not be able to handle.

But none of that ever materialized. I'm not sure why; I think it might be that rescue dogs are somehow grateful. Maybe they know where they've been, so they know how good they have it with us. All I can say is that the dire predictions never came close to being accurate.

One trait Sky unfortunately did not lose was his reaction when strangers approached. He'd start barking wildly at the gardener or the UPS driver or anyone else who tried to invade his territory. If the gardener or another worker was there for two hours, then Sky barked for two hours.

The strange thing about Sky was that when he was out of the house and saw strangers, he was a pussycat. Sky twice tore his ACL, and each time we had to board him at the vet's office while he healed, because he wasn't allowed to be active. The people at the vet's office loved him and thought he was gentle and harmless.

Sky never bit anyone, though in truth we never gave him the opportunity to. But he certainly scared people.

One night close to midnight I was in my office writing, and I heard strange noises that seemed to come from the driveway. It was gated off, so there was no way that our dogs or any outside animals could have gotten in there. I went out to investigate.

Anyone who's read any of my Andy Carpenter books knows that Andy, my alter ego, is a physical coward. But compared to the real-life me, Andy is Davy Crockett.

So I went out to the driveway, which was lit only by moonlight, with considerable trepidation. And the noises I continued to hear moved me toward full-fledged panic. It sounded like there was a fight going on near the end of the driveway, and it included barking and some screeching.

I looked in that direction, and walking toward me was Sky. I had no idea how he could have gotten out there, but that wasn't what I was focusing on.

I was focusing on what was in his mouth.

A dead coyote.

It was maybe thirty-five pounds, so I assume it was a very young coyote. It was remarkable that Sky was able to carry it the way he did, but I really didn't take much time to reflect on his coyote-hauling prowess.

Instead, I screamed "SKY! SKY! SKY!," because in tense situations I am quite the wordsmith. I followed with a few more screams, but Sky kept coming toward me, his prize still in his mouth. Finally, mercifully, he dropped the dead animal, which landed with a disgusting thud and then lay motionless on the ground, just outside our bedroom window.

Sky sauntered the rest of the way toward me, a smile on his face, proud of his accomplishment. I took him into the house so he could brag to his friends, all of whom were barking at the commotion. Debbie was sleeping through the entire thing, but I woke her up and made her look outside the window. I'm not sure what I was trying to accomplish; maybe I just wanted her to share my pain.

In any event, she took a look at it, asked a couple of pertinent questions, such as "How did a dead coyote get in our driveway?," and then went back to sleep.

Sleep was no longer an option for me. Getting the dead coyote out of the driveway in relative darkness was also not an option. Killing myself was the only option I could think of that was still on the table.

So I spent the night in my office, working and surfing the Web. "How to remove a dead coyote from a driveway without touching it" is not a fruitful search on Google.

The other thing I spent the night doing was dreading the morning. It would inevitably become light out—it always did—and I would have to get the damn coyote out of the driveway. It would probably be stiff from rigor mortis, making the prospect even more disgusting.

I was also annoyed. Wasn't this a job for the man of the house? Why wasn't he doing it? I wanted that fictitious person to get me off the hook, because they haven't yet invented the house that I am the man of.

By six A.M. I could no longer pretend that it was still dark. I took a large bath towel out with me and headed down the driveway. When I got within fifty feet of where I knew the coyote was, I turned sideways and inched my way toward it, without looking at it.

My plan, such as it was, was to toss the towel on top of it, without actually seeing it. Then, however I decided to get it out of the driveway, at least I wouldn't have to look at the dead animal.

I admit that it was not a perfect plan, but it might have worked, had the coyote still been there. When I got close enough, I could tell out of the corner of my eye that I was going to be throwing the towel on empty driveway.

This was a mixed blessing. On the positive side, I wouldn't have to perform the dreaded removal operation. More negatively, there was a chance that I was trapped in a gated driveway with a wounded and probably pissed-off coyote . . . the kind of coyote you can't reason with.

Debbie, courageous from the safety of our bedroom window, advised me to look under our car, which was parked in the driveway. That seemed reasonable, so I got as far away from the car as I could, knelt down on the ground, and squinted toward it.

No coyote.

To this day I have no idea how the coyote and Sky got into the driveway in the first place, or how the coyote got out. Someone subsequently told me that coyotes tend to fake their death when they're in danger, but if that was the case in this instance, we had the Robert De Niro of coyotes in our driveway.

All I can say is, for the next six months, I ran to and from the car.

Walking the Dogs

One of our favorite rituals when we lived in Santa Monica was walking the dogs each morning. Of course I would have preferred that Debbie and I each take one and stroll casually along. She preferred that we each take four, and they would pull so much that I'd spend most of the time yelling "Mush!" When we had that many with us, I usually took the less powerful, slightly older ones, because Debbie seemed to have the ability to walk an army.

We worked out a compromise. On days that we planned to stop at Starbucks for coffee and a bagel, we'd take only two dogs each, so that we could sit outside with them comfortably. When we didn't plan to stop, it would be four each.

When we walked the larger group, we attracted a bit of attention, and not only because I was desperately and comically trying to hang on. On at least a half-dozen occasions, cars stopped and the drivers asked for our business card; they assumed we were professional dog walkers. I assured them we were simply professional nutjobs.

One walk in particular is etched in my mind. We took four dogs each, but I wanted to stop at Starbucks anyway. I didn't want to sit there and eat bagels; I really just wanted to hear what the young woman behind the register, Donna, had to say.

The previous night, the first TV movie I had ever written had been broadcast on ABC. It was called *To Love, Honor and Deceive,* and starred Vanessa Marcil. Not a work of art, but pretty good as TV movies go, and I was excited that it had been on.

I was a regular at that Starbucks and had had conversations with Donna in the past. She was a self-described lover of TV movies, and she'd promised to watch mine. I was interested to know what she thought, so I asked Debbie to hang out outside with the eight dogs while I went in and bought muffins for us to take home.

As soon as I came in, Donna started raving about how much she'd loved the movie, how she wanted to see it again, et cetera. The woman in front of me on line clearly had her interest piqued. She asked me what movie we were talking about, and I said, "*To Love, Honor and Deceive.*"

"It was fantastic!" Donna enthused.

"What's it about?" the other woman asked.

It was time for me to be self-deprecating. "It's about two hours."

"No, really."

"Let's put it this way," I said. "You've got your *Citizen Kane,* your *Gone With the Wind,* and your *To Love, Honor and Deceive.*"

Donna moaned, "Oh, I hated *Citizen Kane,*" thus somewhat compromising her position as a reviewer to be respected.

But at least we had the headline for the review ad: "Better than *Citizen Kane!*"—Donna from Starbucks.

I tell that story not because I'm proud of the movie or of Donna's reaction, but because it is the reason I had a bag of muffins in my hand for the rest of our walk.

We always cut across a small park, mainly because the dogs loved watching the squirrels. On this particular day, a squirrel ran in front of us toward a tree. I let the leashes go, which I had done on a few occasions before.

I did that because I knew that the dogs would futilely chase the squirrel to the tree, and it would then run up the tree and peer down at its pursuers, mocking them from its safe perch. There was no possible way that our old dogs could catch the squirrel. Our dogs couldn't catch me.

And this time was no different. The squirrel ran comfortably ahead of the dogs and scurried up the tree. By the time the rest of us got there, the four that I had been walking were looking up at the elusive squirrel and barking like crazy, as if begging it to come down and give them a fighting chance.

Then I heard a scurrying sound from above, and the horror of the next few moments is etched in my memory. The squirrel fell from the tree; it apparently had lost its grip, in a very unsquirrel-like maneuver. And it landed at the feet of the four dogs, none of which could believe their good fortune.

They proceeded to attack it, and I tried to stop them. Debbie tells me that my efforts consisted of hitting the dogs with the bag of Starbucks muffins, all the while screaming "NO! NO! NO!" in a voice about a million octaves higher than my usual voice. She said I sounded like a female opera singer who had swallowed a bug.

And when it was over, the squirrel lay there, wounded but

alive. Debbie ran across the street and rang a doorbell, asking the people who lived there if they had an empty box that we could use. They did, so she ran back with it, scooped the squirrel up, and put it in the box.

We were at Sixth Street, a block east of Wilshire Boulevard, and we knew of a vet on Twelfth and Wilshire. So we ran in a ridiculous procession, Debbie holding on to six dogs, and me with two dogs and a box containing the wounded squirrel.

We barged into the vet's office, and he came out into the reception area to see what the commotion was about. We explained what had happened, and Debbie said that it was important to us that he save the squirrel.

But medical science, or at least that vet, was not up to the task, and he humanely euthanized the squirrel. I left there having learned a valuable lesson: never let four old dogs chase a squirrel, and if you do, make sure you have something a bit heftier than muffins to restore order if necessary.

I have no idea what happened to those muffins, but now I get scones.

They're harder.

Just in case.

Bernie

Bernie is the only Bernese mountain dog we've ever seen in an animal shelter. He was a puppy and didn't have all his markings yet, so I doubt that people knew what he was. We weren't sure ourselves, but we had already fallen in love with the breed when we got Sarah, so we violated our "no puppy" pledge and took him.

He's grown to be a very beautiful, and very large, dog, with a typically great Berner temperament. Debbie would never admit to having a favorite, but he's right up there, just behind Louis.

He tips the scales at an energetic 120 pounds, and sleeps on our bed at night next to Wanda, who dwarfs him at 165. Throw in Jenny and at least one or two others, and our bed can feel fairly crowded.

We've had Bernie for four years as of this writing, and it's in the last six months that he's started to become much more receptive to petting. Prior to this he wouldn't sit still long enough to allow it to happen.

When I wake up during the night, as happens quite often in the asylum that we live in, I look over and Debbie is almost invariably scratching Bernie's stomach. I think she sets her arm to "auto scratch" before she goes to sleep.

When it snows here, Bernie could not be happier. He goes outside and is frequently joined by a bunch of his friends; they all love the cold.

Bernie seemed to enjoy the RV trip, and he is absolutely loving Maine. It would be impossible to imagine a house that he would not brighten.

Final Preparations

For quite a while, Debbie had been mostly disengaged from the actual trip preparations. My best guess is that this was partially due to a misguided notion that I had things under control, and also probably because she was focused on the Maine end of things.

It's difficult to renovate a house from thousands of miles away. Fortunately, we had in Hervochon Construction, people who were extremely competent and totally trustworthy, and that made things easier. But I don't think they, or anyone else we were dealing with there, fully understood the "family" that we were bringing with us, and the accommodations that had to be designed for them.

The dog door was a significant challenge, and then we still had to plan the outside area that the dogs would use when they went through it. A ramp had to be designed to lead there, at an angle that our old, arthritic dogs could manage. And it had to be made of a material that they wouldn't find too slippery in the winter, since we were told they actually had winters in Maine.

Gates needed to be installed on the front porch and rear decks; if the dogs got through an open door, we had to be sure they couldn't run out into the wilderness.

The furniture was another significant issue. Most of our California furniture had been trashed over the years by the dogs, so we had to get new stuff. Debbie used a local store in Maine, Parker Interiors, whose owner, Carolyn Parker, served as a decorator as well.

Debbie spent what seemed like endless hours going over patterns for the chairs and sofas, until finally I had to tell her that none of the material was ever going to be seen. It would all be obscured by slip-covers and sheets to protect it from the dogs; we could do the room in bright red polka dots, and no one would know the difference.

Still, Debbie mostly picked out things that would be nice if ever seen, until we got to the coffee table. We were going to bring our beat-up table with us from California, and Carolyn tried to talk us out of it. Finally, we convinced her by showing her a picture of the table, with Wanda the mastiff and Bernie the Bernese mountain dog sitting on it. There is almost never a time when that table doesn't have a dog on it.

Most important, of course, was that the house be ready when we arrived. We were finding out that there is a different mind-set in Maine than in California; people there are far more mellow and less stressed. Deadlines don't matter quite as much, and people are therefore more flexible and unapologetic about it.

Chris McKenney, our contractor in Maine, called one day to find out if we knew exactly when we'd arrive. This was not a good sign; the house was supposed to be ready for us without question, and now it seemed he was trying to figure out if he had a few extra hours or minutes.

When I expressed concern, he assured me that everything

would definitely be ready, "except for a few things." He said that it was nothing that would affect our being able to live there. A counter wouldn't be installed in the laundry room, the exhaust hood wouldn't be above the range, and the mantel wouldn't yet be over the fireplace.

None of that was a big deal, but I wasn't pleased about the mantel, because it's six hundred pounds and would take a number of people to install. With our dogs, the prospect of having a houseful of workmen was not at all pleasing. "Why won't the mantel be there?" I asked, since it had been ordered a long time before.

"The mantel guy is moose hunting."

I'd already learned that this is how people in Maine talk; they tell you the truth, without hesitation and without apparent embarrassment. In California, they would have fabricated a more legitimate-sounding excuse.

For instance, they might have said, "The stone is coming from Italy, and the craftsmen there took longer to cut it. They're perfectionists, and they'll never change. But believe me, you'll be glad they spent the extra time when you see it." They would say this even if the mantel was being cut in Burbank and looked like it was designed by Mickey Mantle.

Anyway, not to worry, Chris told me, everybody that comes into the house will be comfortable with dogs. And I supposed that was true, if they're comfortable with moose. Or mooses. Or meese.

So Debbie was mostly focused on the Maine end until I took her to examine the RVs we were going to use. That seemed to provide a dose of reality; within two weeks we were going to be boarding these things and living on them for five days.

She started planning the menus for what food we would have onboard. That wasn't great news for me, since she's into eating healthy, while I'm just into eating. So where I would have preferred potato chips, she listed carrots. And my preference for chocolate chip cookies in her version became sugar snap peas. It was a clear difference in philosophy, but I wasn't that worried, since I would be doing the grocery shopping.

She also created the lists of which people and which dogs were going to go into each RV, which I then checked over and edited. Debbie and I would split up; I would be on one of the two large RVs, and she would be on the other. We did it that way so that most of the dogs would have one of us with them, which we knew would keep them calmer.

Once assigned, the dogs would stay on the same RVs the entire trip. It would help us keep track of them; when we called out the roll after each stop, the same seven or nine dogs would bark "Here" on each vehicle.

We agreed that Debbie would put the youngest, most difficult-to-handle dogs on my vehicle, and the easiest on the vehicle that neither of us would be on. Our dogs have very unique relationships with each other, so we knew which ones to split up and which ones to pair together. More thought went into the seating plan for this trip than for most White House state dinners.

The distribution of the humans was easier, and it was based on willingness to drive and experience with a similar type of vehicle. We figured we might have to switch humans occasionally, depending on how tired individual people were, but we'd have flexibility. Not too many people knew each other, and we didn't know everyone, so we didn't let personality figure into our decisions.

We had four real men: Emmit Luther, Randy Miller, Joe Nigro, and Erik Kreider—five if you counted Erik's son, Nick. Emmit and Erik were placed together, and Randy and Joe each went into one of the other vehicles. These were the guys who might have to switch RVs if necessary.

The plan was to drive straight through to Maine, no stopping to sleep. When people weren't driving they could be sleeping or eating or showering or reading or petting or doing whatever they wanted.

We had other rules. Wine and beer were OK to have onboard, but no one would drink any of it within four hours of taking the wheel, and it would only be consumed near the rear of the vehicle. We would always have two people up front; one driving and the other in the passenger seat, making sure that the driver was fresh and awake.

If we got to a point where there weren't six people alert enough to fill those roles, we would stop. No exceptions.

It was all very civilized.

We also went through a process of making sure all the dogs had their shots up-to-date and were taking heartworm medication. Our dogs had never taken heartworm medication before, because heartworm is not a problem in California, but it is to some degree in Maine. Unfortunately, before dogs can take the medication, they must have a blood test to make sure they don't already have the disease. If a dog that already has heartworm takes a heartworm preventative, it will likely be fatal.

So I had to transport twenty-five dogs to the vet, in shifts, to get their blood tests and shots. Trust me when I tell you that it is not a fun process. But by the time I was finished, we had all the paperwork and documents that we could possibly need if stopped by local authorities anywhere. There were no federal laws governing our situation, so we overprepared in case certain states were set up to be difficult.

Finally we were ready. Or maybe not—I had absolutely no idea. The vehicles were huge, and not a single person on the trip had ever driven one. The dogs were great, but how were they going to handle five days on an RV, driving nonstop and surrounded mostly by strangers? The volunteers were enthusiastic; would they stay that way?

For myself, I just wished it were over. Personal comfort is actually not that important to me; I generally don't need to stay in top hotels or fly first class or any of that stuff. But what I do care about is avoiding severe discomfort, and there promised to be a bunch of that on the trip.

E-mails among the group were being exchanged regularly. They were talking about what DVDs they planned to watch, what food they were going to eat, and even what our theme song for the trip should be. I decided that if they started holding hands and singing "Michael, Row the Boat Ashore," I was going to jump off the RV and head for the airport.

But the overriding view of everyone was that it was going to be a great adventure, successful and a hell of a lot of fun.

Except for me.

I was expecting a disaster.

Time to Let Go

My guess is that over the years we've had 300 dogs in our house as pets. I know it's hard to believe, but we have loved each and every one of them in the same way that most people love their one or two pets. We've known their personalities, we've known where each likes to be scratched—we've known each one in a way that most people simply don't think is possible.

As I'm writing this we have 25, which is to say that probably 275 of them have died in our care. Perhaps 10 have passed away at home, usually in their sleep, and we've generally found them in the morning. It's shocking and terrible, but if they've died at home, it usually means that they hadn't shown signs of illness prior to their death. Death came suddenly, and hopefully painlessly.

The remaining 265 have died at a veterinarian's office, which means that we have decided on the appropriate time for their lives to end. It is an awful decision to have to make.

When we first started in rescue, Debbie saw a golden retriever at the West Los Angeles shelter. They estimated his age as fourteen, and he had a leg injury that made it difficult for him to walk. He had been turned in by someone as a stray that they claimed to have found, a ludicrous deception since it was clear that this dog had not jumped over a fence or run away. He could barely go from here to there without falling over.

The shelter people knew that they could never place him, so they were going to euthanize him. Under the circumstances, it was the obvious move for them to make, and I don't blame them at all. But Debbie asked if she could take him to our vet and get a health assessment. If our vet said that he could be made healthy with a reasonable quality of life, then we would have him do so, and we would adopt the dog, which Debbie had already named Buddy.

If our vet said that there was no way to give Buddy that quality of life, then he would put Buddy down, with Debbie there to pet and comfort him during the process.

The shelter, of course, was fine with that, and Debbie took Buddy to our vet. I don't remember all the details, but our vet said that with medication, pain and otherwise, Buddy could certainly be healthy enough to enjoy the time he had left. The vet estimated that time to be about six months.

So we took Buddy home, and he blossomed. He enjoyed interacting with the other dogs, though he certainly didn't partake in the wrestling matches that spontaneously broke out. But he watched them from a distance and smiled a lot and ate really well. There was not a single day that we had any regret about the decision to rescue him.

The vet was off on his timing by a month, unfortunately in the wrong direction. After five months, it was like Buddy fell off a cliff. He stopped eating, didn't want to get up, and disengaged from the other dogs.

So we took him back to the vet, who confirmed that Buddy had reached the end.

As I described with Tara, the normal euthanasia process is for the vet to use a mild sedative to calm the dog down. Then he shaves an area on the leg to make it easier to get to a vein, and he administers a vial of pink liquid through a syringe. This is what he did with Buddy, and Debbie and I comforted Buddy and petted him throughout the process.

Debbie and I try to always both be there when we have to put a dog down, but sometimes it isn't possible, and only one of us is able to pet and provide comfort. When we are both there, she usually pets the dog on the head and whispers in his or her ear. I do the petting on the dog's back and side, and we both keep it up until the vet checks for a heartbeat and tells us that it's over.

Since it was early in our rescue lives, we were very, very upset by what had taken place with Buddy. Not Tara upset, but certainly emotionally drained.

But that night we came to terms with it and developed a point of view that we've tried to find comfort in ever since. What we needed to focus on was that for whatever time we had Buddy or any other dog, he or she was safe and happy and loved.

That was all we could do, and it would have to be good enough, or we'd go insane. I say this knowing full well that most people would look at our life with dogs and decide that we've already opted for the "go insane" route.

People write to me all the time for advice about when to euthanize. They confuse my being a dog lunatic with my being a dog expert. Sometimes they're facing the dreaded decision and are worried that they might make the wrong one. Just as often they've already made the decision and gone ahead with the euthanasia, and belatedly fear that they've done something wrong.

I'm very reluctant to offer any kind of counsel. First of all, I don't know their dog and haven't seen the situation firsthand. I know only what they're telling me, and that could easily be colored by the emotional state that they're obviously in.

I'm also not a vet, although sometimes I feel like one, since among other things I probably give out sixty pills a day for various ailments. But I don't want to recommend to people that they put their dog down when in fact it might have an ailment that a vet could easily cure. Nor do I want to recommend that they keep it alive, since perhaps that would be prolonging incurable suffering.

The overriding point is that I'm not in their home, and I certainly can't attempt to evaluate the situation from a distance. I wouldn't even feel comfortable doing it from up close; it is a personal decision that they have to arrive at themselves, with the counsel of their vet.

So all I can do is give them the benefit of my experience, and tell them how we've evolved on the subject.

In the case of Tara, I feel we waited too long. We took extraordinary measures to prolong her life, but in retrospect I think that was more for us than for her, though that is certainly not how we viewed it at the time.

I think we should have let her go sooner, but hopefully we have learned from our mistake.

The most important clue, in my eyes, is whether the dog is eating. Now, I don't mean to say that if it's not eating that means its life should be ended; I mean it in reverse. If a dog is in bad pain or feeling miserable, it will not eat. So I don't think we have ever made a decision to euthanize a dog that was eating well.

The other rule we go by is less well defined. It involves dignity, and our absolute refusal to let a dog lose it. If a dog can't get up on its own, if it is urinating on itself, those are the kinds of things that involve a loss of dignity in our eyes, and we just don't think that's fair to the dog.

But it's almost always a tough call, and the bottom line is quality of life. I got a call once from a woman in Palm Springs who had heard about us through another rescue group. She had a golden named Winnie, only one and a half years old, who had a tumor on her leg. The woman had neither the money nor the inclination to deal with it, and she asked us if we would take Winnie.

I drove out and picked up just about the sweetest, most beautiful dog I had ever seen. She was blond and thin and had a perpetual smile on her face. She also had a tumor on her leg the size of a softball.

I took her right to our vet, who told me that the tumor was obviously cancerous, and so large that it could not be removed. The only solution was amputation of the leg, and even that would not do the trick. A bone cancer that advanced would have already started to spread, and it was going to kill Winnie, one way or the other.

The question we most often ask our vets is what they would do in a situation if it was their dog that was ill or injured. In Winnie's case, he surprised me by saying he would amputate the leg.

I pushed back, especially since he said the amputation would probably give her only six to eight months of continued

comfortable life. Wouldn't most of that time be spent adjust-
ing to having only three legs? I asked. Why put her through
that difficulty for such a short time?

He made his case, and at the end of the day, we trusted him.
We had Winnie's leg amputated, and the result was amazing.
Within forty-eight hours, she was up and around, running on
the three legs better than most dogs do on four. I've never
seen anything like it.

Her energy level was sky-high; after all, she was little more
than a puppy. She wrestled with the other dogs, fetched tennis
balls, and loved every second that she had.

Those seconds added up to about ten months. When she
got sick it happened all at once, and she really did not suffer at
all. Giving her that extra time was as good a decision as we've
ever made; Winnie made the most of it.

The best advice I can give is to try your best to think only
of the dog and its quality of life. In most cases, if a loving dog
owner is struggling with the decision, then it's probably time
to let the dog go, because those are the kinds of owners that
look for reasons to delay and deny. It's human nature.

Sometimes you get it right and sometimes you get it wrong.
All you can do is your best.

Evie

One day I got home and there was a message on the answering machine from Ron Edwards of the SEACCA animal shelter. The message was simple; he had a Saint Bernard named Evie that we simply had to take.

We had complete confidence in Ron's ability to pick worthy dogs, and we had always wanted a Saint Bernard, so we headed for the shelter, which was in Downey, immediately.

Rescue people can be a little over the top and demanding of potential adopters, which is why they're sometimes disparaged as "rescue Nazis." But if there is one given, it is that once someone rescues a dog, that dog is officially under that person's protection, and that trust will not be violated.

Debbie and I took it a step further. We considered the dog under our protection once we decided in our own mind that we would take it, even if we hadn't yet done so.

A typical example of this would be our getting a phone call

alerting us to a golden in a shelter that needed saving. It could have come at a time when we were overcrowded and had no space to take in a new dog. But since we would never leave a golden in a shelter under any circumstances, we would immediately pick the dog up.

Once we got to the shelter, though, we might find that it wasn't a golden after all, but instead maybe a mixed breed that might have been 5 percent golden. It didn't matter by that point; it could have been a giraffe and we would still have taken it, because the dog was mentally under our protection the moment we decided to go to the shelter. To then turn our backs on it because it was a mix would be the same in our minds as if we euthanized it ourselves.

Evie presented a slightly different dilemma. She *was* a Saint Bernard, and an adorable one at that, but she had a couple of other issues. For one, she was eight years old, which is very old for that breed, and she had some health problems. That in itself would not have been significant, except for the fact that one of the issues was that she was blind.

We've had blind dogs in our house on a number of occasions, and it's remarkable how they adapt. They say you shouldn't move the furniture around when you have a blind animal, but we had an average of thirty four-legged "pieces of furniture" walking around all the time. Yet blind dogs always seemed to be able to navigate the situation. And they would do it with a smile.

But Evie was huge, and not that mobile in the first place. We had a real concern about her ability to handle things, and we hated the thought of putting her through the stress that her new surroundings would involve if she wasn't going to be happy.

On the other hand, not taking her would mean she'd stay in the shelter for a few more days and then get euthanized, because there was zero chance someone else was going to show up to adopt an elderly, blind Saint Bernard. Ron knew that as well as we did, and he had fallen in love with her, which is why he'd called us.

So we took her home. We could have used a crane to get her in and out of the car, but none was available, so we managed ourselves. And then came the scary part: introducing her to the group. They mobbed her, as they always do, and she handled it really well.

I can't imagine what might have been in her mind, unable to see these hordes of lunatics coming over to check her out, but she just stood there stoically and waited them out. They weren't intimidated by her size, and she wasn't intimidated by their number or energy. It was a stalemate, which was welcome news and a good start.

It's often fascinating to watch dogs' personalities evolve once they're in our house, at least as it relates to dealing with our crew. Over time they become more comfortable, and their true nature comes out, often in unpredictable ways.

With Debbie and me, Evie was totally sweet and loving; if I've ever met a dog that liked petting more, I can't remember it. She would hear us walking toward her and would lower her head slightly so as to be in the petting-receiving position.

She was somewhat less tolerant of her canine friends, however. It's not that she was aggressive toward them; it was more that she wanted nothing to do with them. She staked out a place in the corner of the living room, where we laid a dog bed, to be her permanent place of residence.

We called it "Evie's Island," and good luck to the dog that had the temerity to try and enter. Evie would sense their presence and growl angrily as a warning. If that didn't do the trick,

Tara — The Greatest Dog in the History of the World.

With Randy Miller — There's one real man at that table, and it isn't me.

Little Sara graciously sharing her couch with Benji and Terri Nigro.

Little Sara — not sharing her couch with anyone.

Bumper — Louisville to New Mexico to California to Maine . . . that dog gets around.

Wanda and Bumper — Just before we took Vegas by "storm."

Feeding time — "Grassy area for two? Right this way, please."

Joe Nigro and Emmit Luther getting the fencing ready.

Cyndi Flores and Terri Nigro preparing a delicious meal.

Sally — Compared to life with a hoarder in the Mojave Desert, this is a piece of cake.

Mamie — Only wanted to sit on the couches, but had to be hoisted up each time.

Benji — Always alert and ready for whatever . . .

George Kentris with Louis, Otis, and Kahlani — George was truly there when we needed him.

Comfort Inn in Findlay, Ohio — George's hotel was an oasis for us.

Bumper — "Just let me know when we get there . . . until then I want to sleep."

Jack — "Why is no one petting me?"

Big Sarah — Never stops smiling.

Ready to load up in California.

Noel and Jack — Loving life.

Wanda, the gentle giant — Her mission was to cover the entire RV with slobber.

Emmit Luther — Without Emmit, Randy, and Joe, we'd probably still be in Nebraska.

Nick Kreider with Jack and Noel — Nick was petting the entire way.

Me with part of the gang — telling them not to shed in the RV's.

Cindy Spodek Dickey, Cyndi Flores, Terri Nigro, and Mary Lynn Dundas — Smiling every single second of the trip, and I still have no idea why.

A brief unsuccessful attempt at sleep.

she'd bark and snap at them, and she had to do it only once. The offending dog would immediately retreat back across the imaginary causeway, never to return.

Fortunately, Evie was house-trained, so she would leave the island to go out to the yard a couple of times a day. Suffice it to say that the other dogs cleared a path for her to walk; nobody was inclined to mess with Miss Evie.

One day we were babysitting a friend's golden retriever, Lincoln. The friend had adopted Lincoln from us not long before and didn't want to put him in a boarding facility when he went on vacation, so we took him in to stay with us.

Debbie was out of the house and I was working in my office when Lincoln unwisely ventured onto Evie's Island. I didn't see it happen, but I heard the scream and came running. Lincoln had made a rookie mistake, and the irascible Evie had reacted to the invasion by biting his ear off.

Actually, I'm exaggerating; I only thought that was what had happened. It turned out that she hadn't bitten the ear entirely off; she'd just torn it some. But it created a huge amount of blood, especially since Lincoln was shaking his head with the pain, thereby spraying the blood around the room.

I grabbed Lincoln and ran with him to the car, and we were off to the vet's office. It turned out to be a much less serious injury than I had feared, and the vet quickly sewed him up, assuring me that the ear would be as good as new in a couple of weeks.

In the meantime, Debbie had come home and seen the blood everywhere. It looked like *The Texas Chain Saw Massacre* had been filmed in the place. I wasn't home, so there was no way for her to know what happened, and in her panic she couldn't tell if any dogs were missing.

So she frantically called the various vets that we dealt with to find out if I had brought in an emergency case. She ultimately tracked me down while Lincoln was having his ear repaired, and I assured her that everything was fine.

And then it hit me. Debbie had been calling animal hospitals, not human ones. How did she know the blood wasn't mine? I was missing, and it's not like she'd conducted a DNA test to determine that the blood was canine in origin. How did she know I wasn't in some emergency room somewhere, being prepped for surgery?

I pointed this out to her in an effort to make her feel guilty, an effort that as far as I could tell was completely unsuccessful.

So maybe there was a lesson in all of that for me; I'm not sure. But there certainly was a lesson for the dogs.

Nobody, but nobody, was to enter Evie's Island.

Mamie and Coki

When I was in Houston at a signing event for Golden Beginnings Rescue, Debbie e-mailed me to say that the East Valley shelter in the San Fernando Valley had called to tell her that there was a ten-year-old golden scheduled to be put down that afternoon. She was letting me know that she was heading over there to rescue it.

I knew exactly what this meant; Debbie shops in animal shelters the way most people shop in malls. She points and says, "I want that one, and that one, and that one . . ."

She got four dogs that day. The golden, which she named Mamie; Wanda, the mastiff; Luke, a black Lab mix; and Coki, a border collie mix. Luke died well before we made the trip to Maine, but Coki and Mamie joined Wanda on the RVs.

I don't think Mamie is a purebred golden—there's probably a little chow in her—but she's close. She hangs out at the top of the steps in the Maine house, sleeping on the landing, and it gives her a view out onto her world. Except for Sara the beagle, Mamie is probably the most demanding dog we have; she wants to eat on her schedule and will not accept any excuses.

She also demands her own water dish, and would rather die of thirst than drink from the other water dishes, the ones the peasants use.

Coki is scraggly looking but adorable, with a smile on her face twenty-four hours a day. She is completely unintimidated by her housemates, even though most of them outweigh her by anywhere from thirty to a hundred pounds.

I left my closet door open one day, and Coki curled up in there. It remained her base of operations until about three months after our arrival in Maine. She took ill one morning, and the vet discovered an inoperable tumor on her liver, which ended her life.

Mamie and Wanda are therefore sadly the lone remaining witnesses to Debbie's shopping spree.

The Gang Was All There

We'd flown in everyone that needed flying, which consisted of five people. Cyndi Flores came in from Virginia, Emmit Luther from Atlanta, Randy Miller from Houston, Cindy Spodek Dickey from Seattle, and Mary Lynn Dundas from Northern California. Erik and Nick Kreider, Terri and Joe Nigro, and of course Debbie and I were Southern California–based.

Everybody had arrived, which to me was counterintuitive. If I had been them, I would have parachuted out of the plane long before it got anywhere near us.

We put them all up at a hotel in Costa Mesa, near the RV place, and we set up a dinner, which would serve as a get-acquainted/last-minute-planning session. Everybody seemed normal, which was another surprise, since normal people wouldn't be doing this.

Of course, it was possible that I was making judgments about human generosity and caring based on my own views on the subject, which was not a very informed view. I resolved to spend some time on the trip observing the humans, to better understand the race.

The dinner was amazingly pleasant. No one was showing any trepidation at all, with the obvious exception of yours truly. All of them seemed very comfortable with one another, laughing and joking and all expressing eagerness to start on the adventure.

Mary Lynn was the only person in the group that I hadn't ever spoken to; she had signed on through Cyndi Flores. Like everyone else, she seemed extraordinarily pleasant and accommodating, expressing a willingness to do whatever was necessary on the trip.

She described to me the night she and Cyndi were sitting on her porch and Cyndi told her about the trip. She had accurately pointed out that it was totally crazy and then asked to be included. She had been a lover of dogs her entire life, so she relished the prospect of being literally surrounded by them. She actually thought it was a great opportunity, and she thanked me for including her.

Maybe I was mistaken; maybe we had flown these people in from Mars.

Debbie gave a toast, welcoming everyone and expressing our extreme gratitude for all that they were doing. It was really quite remarkable and selfless, because by any standard, five days on the road without stopping can be arduous and tiring. Add twenty-five dogs to the mix, and I can say with total certainty that even if all went well, it would be exhausting. Everybody understood this, but no one seemed worried or put off by it.

I remember looking around the table and marveling at what was happening. In terms of time and energy, they were doing a more substantial favor for us than I had ever done for anyone in my life. And they barely knew us!

I've since asked them why they did it, and they've pretty much unanimously said that it wasn't only for the dogs, it was also for us. But the reason they considered us worthy of it was because of what they knew we had done for dogs.

It was the "power of the paw."

The plan was to all meet the next day at the RV place at two o'clock, the earliest the vehicles would be ready. We had hoped to get them earlier, but the people who were renting them didn't have to have them back until noon.

Once we got them, we'd drive the thirty minutes to our house, where we'd load up the supplies first, and then the dogs. My hope was that we could be on the road to Maine by five o'clock.

I went a little nuts buying food . . . twenty-five pounds of cold cuts for sandwiches, many fruit platters, every kind of snack and drink imaginable. Mary Lynn's son, a chef, had prepared two elaborate Italian dinners that we were going to take along and have the first and second nights.

We picked up the vehicles, a process that took about an hour longer than we had scheduled. The proprietor, not exactly a high-energy guy, gave a brief, listless run-through on how the RVs work. I didn't even bother to listen, since our real men were on the case.

Emmit took the wheel of the first RV and led the procession as I directed us on the half-hour trip to our house. We quickly ran into our first difficulty. We lived at the top of a hill, on a small private road. There was no way to get the huge RVs up the hill, and even if there was, we'd never be able to turn around. The road near our house was simply too narrow.

So, with the help of our great neighbors, Diane and Ralph Lee and Mary Ellen and Laurie Park, we ran a shuttle of supplies down from the house to the RVs at the bottom of the hill. There was a lot of stuff; human food and dishes, dog food and dishes, pots and pans, coffeemakers, linens, fencing, and much more.

Debbie had bought so much toilet paper that I think we could *have wiped each dog's ass after they did their business throughout the trip.*

After the supplies came the dogs, who had absolutely no idea what was going on or who these strangers were. But everybody started petting them, so the dogs calmed down and were fine with it. Not that I had any doubts before, but it became more dramatically clear what dog lovers our volunteers were. They were going to have to be.

The scene was very chaotic, made more so by the fact that local Orange County media people had found out about it and were there to take pictures and interview us.

The interviewer put a camera in my face and asked what we were going to do if the dogs drooled. "We're used to it," I said.

It was eight o'clock and dark out before we took off. I knew that could cause us a problem of sorts on the other end. We'd taken over a bed-and-breakfast place, Damariscotta Lake Farm, which is near our house in Maine, for the Thursday night when we arrived, but that was based on a very optimistic schedule. Being three hours behind before we even left was not a promising start toward keeping that schedule.

Emmit was driving the vehicle I was on, along with Erik and Nick Kreider. Debbie was accompanied by Cindy Spodek Dickey, as well as Joe and Terri Nigro, with Joe behind the wheel. On the smallest of the three vehicles were the remaining three humans: Cyndi Flores, Mary Lynn Dundas, and Randy Miller. Randy was doing the driving. We'd set it up so that for the first leg, we had "real men" in the driver's seat, which meant I was in the passenger's seat.

There were nine dogs in my RV, nine in Debbie's, and seven in the smaller one. I couldn't even imagine what was going through their minds; it was an amazing upheaval in their lives. They seemed to be handling it well, and, as they do in the house, quickly found comfortable places to sack out. The shaking and rattling of the vehicles, while disconcerting to me, seemed to have a soothing effect on them.

I tried to tune the radio to Monday Night Football. I don't think I'd ever missed a Monday Night Football game in my life; it is vital for me in that it helps bridge the terrifying gap between the NFL on Sunday and a full college slate the following Saturday.

But the radio was awful; it was impossible to hear anything. Not an auspicious beginning, but I took comfort in the fact that by the next Monday I would be watching the game in front of a roaring fireplace in our house in Maine.

Or so I hoped.

In any event, we were off.

Annie

I was in the San Fernando Valley to pick up a golden retriever at the West Valley animal shelter. Shelters knew us, since we were there all the time, and after some training they were semi-programmed to call us whenever a golden came in. It was hit or miss, but it improved gradually over time.

While I was there, a kennel worker named Denise called me over. I knew her only to nod hello, and I don't think we'd ever had a conversation more substantive than discussing what a dog's age might be or whether it had the mange.

We went into a back office, and within moments she was sobbing. At that moment I would have rather been on Pluto than in that office. Her sobbing caused me to feel sympathy, as much for me as for her.

Nevertheless, I asked her what was wrong. I don't know if she heard the question, but it didn't matter, because she was going to tell me anyway.

Once she composed herself, at least for the moment, she told me about Annie, a one-and-a-half-year-old shepherd/collie mix. Annie had come in seven weeks before, which surprised me, since dogs generally did not last nearly that long in that shelter if they weren't adopted.

But there was a good reason that Annie had stayed alive. Annie had come in with a badly broken leg, which would under normal circumstances have ensured her quick demise. There was no way the shelter would have the inclination or the resources to have a vet fix the leg, since the injury would probably kill any chances she'd have of getting adopted. So, they would reason, why spend the money on a dog that would eventually be euthanized anyway?

But Denise fell in love with Annie, in a way that she said had never happened before. Shelter workers are generally caring people who like dogs as well as anyone else. I don't know how they deal with watching what happens to so many of them, but I guess they just shut themselves off to it.

But Denise couldn't shut Annie off.

In order to keep her alive, she started moving her around to different cages, fixing it so that each time, the record showed that she was a new dog, having just arrived. My guess is that the records system within the shelter is not without its flaws, and Denise used the inefficiency to put off Annie's euthanasia.

She managed to do that for five weeks, at which point her bosses caught on, and the dog jig, as they say, was up. But Denise was not about to fail, and she took Annie out of the shelter and to a nearby vet.

But Denise had no money, and the vet was refusing to operate without getting paid, so Annie just sat there with her broken leg, in a cage, for going on two weeks. It was driving

Denise crazy, and she had nowhere else to turn, so she was turning to us.

She knew we concentrated on golden retrievers and other larger dogs, but would we take Annie?

If ever there was a no-brainer, the decision of whether to rescue Annie was it. Her situation defined the reason for rescue; to refuse her would be to not belong in the field. So of course I said yes.

But we would not be having the vet that kept the injured Annie stuck in a cage for two weeks fix the leg. We took her to our surgeon, who x-rayed it and told us that the break was really bad, and that the situation was further complicated by the long delay since the injury happened.

He would do the surgery, but he'd have to put in a metal plate to make sure the bones healed correctly. Annie would then have to spend another six weeks in a cage at his office, since she couldn't engage in any activity that might put stress on the leg. At his office they could keep her immobile and monitor her in a way that we could not.

She came through the surgery well and took up residence in her new cage. Debbie and I visited her regularly, but we couldn't take her for walks, since that might endanger her healing. So we sat with her and petted her and gave her some biscuits.

I bonded with her during that period, and eventually I had to stop visiting because she'd get so excited when she saw me that she'd try to jump up and down. Finally the six weeks were up, and we could take her out of there and set about finding her a home. Denise couldn't take her, much as she wanted to, because she was already over the limit in her apartment, and her landlord was threatening to evict her.

Debbie and I had a dilemma. Usually we would have

brought her to the vet's office where we boarded the dogs await-
ing adoption. But it just felt too cruel to put her in still another
cage, so instead we took her home. She was obviously too
young and healthy to qualify as one of our "at home" dogs, but
she'd stay there while we found her a permanent home.

When a potential adopter would want to see her, we'd
bring Annie to meet them at the vet's office. We felt it would be
easier for her to bond with new people outside our home. This
way the people could meet her on neutral territory, take her for
a walk, pet her, and get to know her.

It didn't work out so well.

Annie simply wanted nothing to do with any of them. She
wouldn't walk on the leash, always trying to drag them to where
she thought I was waiting. If they tried to force her, she bared
her teeth and growled at them, a sure way to kill any chance at
adoption.

So we finally gave in to the obvious; Annie had been through
a lot, and she was not going to let her journey end at any house
other than ours. She had already made friends with the other
dogs, and that was where she was going to live. As far as I could
tell, her decision was final.

Of the three hundred or so dogs that we've had in our
home as pets, I can give you an exact count of how many have
preferred me to Debbie.

Three.

And Annie was one of them.

She was absolutely devoted to me; there was not a moment
that I was home that she was not by my side. At the time, five
dogs slept in bed with Debbie and me, and she was one of them,
because she was one of the few young and athletic enough to
jump onto the bed without assistance. But she wouldn't get on

the bed until I did; and when she did we literally shared a pillow, weird as that might sound.

She was my pal and my protector, and the feelings were very, very mutual.

Annie lived for thirteen years with us, and she died after a short illness. It was for me one of the toughest losses I've faced, and by definition, I've faced a lot of them. I held her in the vet's office when she died, as I always did, and the best way I can describe it is that it was exquisitely painful.

I was losing a friend, a living, feeling being that had loved me unconditionally for every day that she lived with us. So that was as hard as you would expect—maybe harder. But I also reflected on where she had been, and how she had amazingly overcome it all to have a long and happy life.

It also showed me how dog rescue, like most everything else, is totally dependent on luck and being in the right or wrong place at the right or wrong time.

Had I not happened to get a call that day about a golden retriever, I would never have heard about or adopted Annie. I have no doubt that she would have died in that vet's cage, probably at the end of a needle.

But Denise stepped up and gave a damn, I got the call, and it all worked out. And I know that in the majority of cases it doesn't work out, but I want to celebrate when it does.

Annie was something to celebrate.

She missed going to Maine by about two years. She would have loved it, because she always loved wherever she was and whatever she was doing. The smile on her face and the wag of her tail proved it.

I will always feel good about that.

And I will always miss her.

Idiots

We've dealt with a lot of them in our time in rescue. They are the owners who dump their dogs into situations knowing that the dogs will not survive. They think of them as possessions, and it doesn't bother them to discard the dogs any more than it would to discard an old car.

That is not to say that there aren't circumstances in which someone simply cannot keep a dog. Economics, illness or death in the family, a change in living circumstances . . . all of those things can make dog ownership difficult or impossible. But that doesn't mean you just throw out the dog without providing for its protection as best you can.

Dogs have feelings; anybody who spends five minutes with one has to know that. They feel fear and love and gratitude and joy and anger and much more. But there are some people, many people, who either don't understand that or don't care.

There is a name for those people.

Assholes.

As a rescue group, we usually tried to avoid taking a dog from an owner who wanted to get rid of it. Our theory was and is that those dogs at least had their owner to protect them, while the dogs in the shelter had no one. If the owner did not live up to his or her responsibility and dumped the dog in a shelter, then it would become a candidate for our rescue. But not until then.

The exceptions to this rule were golden retrievers. We made a posthumous promise to Tara that we would always take a golden, for any reason, at any time.

So it was that we got Reggie.

Reggie was an eight-year-old golden that was going to be put into a shelter by his owner if we didn't take him. So of course we said that we would, and the owner showed up with his girlfriend and Reggie.

As we always did, we asked the owner why he was giving Reggie up. He explained, without apparent embarrassment, that he liked to go running every morning with his dog. For years Reggie had happily obliged, but now, at eight years old, Reggie simply couldn't keep up anymore.

So it was time to get another dog.

You don't want to tell such people what you think of them, for fear that they will not then give you their dog. It was easy for me to hold my tongue in such situations anyway, since I am not a fan of confrontation.

My task was to keep Debbie in check, and it was a difficult one in the case of Reggie's owner. I prevailed only by asking her if she wanted to risk this dope's leaving and taking Reggie with him, to who knows where.

So we got Reggie, with the intention of placing him in a home. He would stay in a dog run at the vet until he got adopted.

But first he would get checked out physically and get a much-needed bath.

He checked out fine, and then Debbie put him in the tub to give him the bath. Midway through it, she called me over and said that she needed to run a quick errand, and asked if I could finish the bath and put Reggie into the cage. She'd be back in twenty minutes to pick me up so that we could go home.

It was diabolical. Debbie knew full well that ten minutes alone with Reggie would result in my absolute refusal to put him in the cage. He had these intense eyes that looked right through you, and a quiet dignity that goldens possess in amazing abundance.

And while I was bathing him, he licked my face.

Game, set, and match.

When Debbie came back, I was sitting on a couch in the reception area with Reggie on my lap, and she just laughed and said, "Let's go."

Reggie lived with us for four years, and I can honestly say that there has never been a better dog than him, Tara included. In his last six months, we learned that he loved to lick the bowl of Cherry Garcia frozen yogurt after I had some. Soon I would leave a scoop of it behind so that he could do more than lick the edges.

Just as in Tara's honor we no longer eat hot dogs, in Reggie's we no longer eat Cherry Garcia. Can't we find a dog that loves spinach?

Reggie's death was comparatively easy on him, with a minimum of pain. He was doing really well, and then he woke up one morning unable to move. It was a cancer of the spine, and we had to put him down that day. There was really no decision to be made, and he barely suffered at all. I wish it always happened like that.

But of course it was tough on us. I cried when Reggie was euthanized, a rarity for me. It's just a hard thing to process, that we were making a conscious decision to destroy this living creature that we loved. It wasn't that we had doubts about what we were doing; the vet said that Reggie would die either way. We were simply hastening the process and removing the terrible suffering.

When this happens, I can only hope that the dogs understand, that they know we are protecting them, just as surely as we were protecting them when they were healthy. But there's no way to know, and it really couldn't change our decision even if we did.

If we had a "ring of honor" of dogs that were our absolute favorites, Reggie would certainly be included. Along with Tara and Charlie and Sophie and Joey and Rocky and Harry and Weasel and . . . let's just say we'd need a really big ring.

The day after Reggie died, four years after we got him, the owner's girlfriend called us. I don't even know how she tracked us down, but she told us that what the guy did had bothered her for four years, and she had always wanted to know what had happened to Reggie.

I told her about the great four years Reggie had with us, and how much we loved him. I also told her the bad news from the day before, and she started crying. I never did ask her if she was still dating the loser.

Sometimes the idiots are anonymous. We got a call once from the Downey shelter about a fourteen-year-old golden in their possession. That is very old for a golden, and for it to be stuck in a shelter like that at that age was absolutely unacceptable.

When we got there, we heard the full story. The dog had been tied up in front of the shelter before they opened, and the morons who left her there had attached a note to her collar.

It said that her name was Tessie, that she was fourteen years old, and that she had been a great dog. But the people were going on vacation and didn't want to pay to board her, so they were asking the shelter to put her down for them.

They don't come lower than that.

So we took Tessie, who was in excellent health, and she immediately became the imperious Queen Mother of the house. She was cantankerous, as befitted her age, and was above interaction with the other dogs—the "commoners." She wasn't very large, but she ate like a horse, and she starting barking impatiently a half hour before each feeding time.

She lived for four years, to the grand old age of eighteen. We think that's the oldest golden we've ever had, though it's hard to know for sure. In her case we knew her age because of the note, but generally we had no such information on dogs we would rescue. Still, I doubt that any of them lived to eighteen.

But most of them had one thing in common with Tess and Reggie.

Their previous owners were dumb as dirt.

Bart

A rescue person contacted us once and told us about a golden retriever she had seen in the San Bernardino shelter. She was in a run with a black Lab mix, and when she was there, both dogs were coughing. Kennel cough is quite common in Los Angeles area shelters, and often it is a sign of much worse, so I got down there as soon as I could.

It wasn't soon enough. The golden had died, and the black Lab mix, which the shelter had named Maverick, was quite ill. I rescued him and took him to our vet, who immediately put him on a regimen of powerful antibiotics and told me that it was fifty-fifty that he'd make it.

He made it, and after a month in the hospital came home. Debbie had renamed him Bart, and he fit right in with the gang. He sleeps in the middle of the living room, which along with my office is the area of highest dog density. But he really shows little interest in interacting with them; it's more like he's dogwatching.

All of our dogs except for Louis are frequent barkers, but Bart puts them to shame. He'll start barking before six in the morning, with periodic outbursts throughout the day. If we pet him, even briefly, he will stop. If we didn't, I don't think he'd ever stop. He's the only one of our dogs that doesn't bark as a result of some event or visitor or noise or other dog doing it.

Bart barks because Bart barks.

He seems fine with that.

You Know the Old Saying . . .

. . . a trip hasn't officially started until Weasel has thrown up.

Based on that maxim, it took about ten minutes for our trip to officially begin. I heard gagging and retching near the back of the RV, a sound that I was all too familiar with. It sounded like Weasel, but I couldn't be sure.

We'd anticipated all kinds of dog accidents in the vehicles, and Debbie had brought along enough cleaning supplies to disinfect the Everglades. They were about to get their first test.

I was in the passenger seat, and with all the dogs lying everywhere it was not an easy place to navigate in and out of. Based on the maneuverability inside the vehicle, I expected to have my fifth back surgery by the time we reached Vegas.

"Someone threw up back there," I said, stating the obvious and starting to get up. It would have been above and beyond the call of duty for me to expect Erik or Nick to jump up to clean it, and Emmit was driving, so he was off the hook.

"I got it," Nick said, endearing himself to me for the rest of our natural lives. He grabbed a plastic bag and a towel and headed toward the back to deal with it. Maybe the trip wasn't going to be so bad after all.

Our RV was leading the way, and Emmit started out by driving fairly slowly and cautiously. I think he just wanted to make sure that the drivers behind him were comfortable keeping up, and they seemed to be doing just fine. Within fifteen minutes we were on the 15 headed north, and we'd increased our speed. It seemed almost surreal that after all the planning, we were finally on the open road, heading to our destination.

The first leg of the trip was toward Vegas, a drive I had made many times in my normal role of gambling degenerate. Jean, Nevada, is not too far from Vegas. I actually know something about the place, since I used it as a scene in one of my books. In the book, someone was murdered in a Jean casino parking lot, but I decided not to point that out to my traveling companions.

There are actually no citizens of Jean. It's simply a couple of casino hotels, positioned to attract gamblers who can't wait to get to Vegas or want one last chance to break even on the way out. The hotels are much tackier than those in Vegas, and not even as nice as those in Primm, a similar town we had passed about fifteen minutes before.

Jean was going to be our experimental first stop. We pulled into a rest area, and Randy, Joe, and Emmit jumped out to figure out the best way to handle things. They had an air about them that said they knew what they were doing, which under the circumstances was comforting.

Randy decided we should pull the vehicles nose to rear, so that they were lined up with almost no space between them.

Then we got the fencing out from the storage area under one of the vehicles and started to unfurl it. It began at the front of the lead RV, and we made a half-circle, ending at the rear of the last one. However, Randy then realized that the dogs might still go under the RVs and could then run off through the back, without being confined by the fence. So we extended the perimeter behind the RVs to make a complete circle; I was glad we'd brought as much fence as we had.

Emmit and Joe walked the length of the fence, making sure that the stakes were driven solidly into the ground. Then a few people positioned themselves along the outside of the fence, confirming that it was secure and able to resist the potential onslaught of dogs, who would no doubt be energetic and very excited to get off their mobile homes. Then the rest of us started to help the dogs make their way out, one vehicle at a time.

It actually went fairly well, but it was a time-consuming process. Most of the dogs are old and if left to their own devices would have had difficulty navigating the steep steps, so they had to be helped or carried. Others bounded off eagerly, and they had to be held back and calmed down lest they plow through the fairly fragile fence.

I had fed the dogs at the house before we left, so we didn't need to do that again this night. Instead we just gave out some biscuits, and let them wander around until they did their business.

Debbie led the "shit patrol" around the area; she is an efficient genius with a plastic bag. It was mostly the women who joined her in the task, and they armed themselves with plastic bags of their own to scavenge the area. If it had been up to me, I don't know that I'd have been so neat about the whole thing, but they actually left the area in pretty much the same condition as we found it.

Then we started to load the dogs back on the RVs, and I quickly *discovered that getting them up the steps was a little tougher than getting them down. I think it was a gravity thing.*

We had lists as to who went where, and we did a double count to make sure that each dog was accounted for. There was no evidence that any had gotten outside the fence, but we wanted to be completely sure. I'm always a little neurotic about stuff like that, so even when the people on each RV reported that all their dogs were on board, I got on and did a quick count of my own.

Once that was accomplished, we rolled the fence back up and stored it away. The process had taken close to an hour, which was more than I would have liked. Hopefully we'd get faster as we did it more frequently. If not, a long trip had just gotten a lot longer.

We pulled into a gas station in Jean and got jolted by the fact that it cost about $150 to fill up each vehicle. This was not a good sign, since we'd barely left home. I'm good at math, but I opted not to do the calculations on what it was going to cost to get to Maine. I was depressed enough.

Even if we were able to buy enough gas to make it to Maine, we were not going to be a fitter group by the time we arrived. That became obvious when the non-canine members of our team made a beeline for the convenience store attached to the gas station.

Everybody came out of there with hot dogs, chips, nachos, and pretty much every unhealthy food item ever invented. Apparently, the cold cuts and fruit that I had purchased held very little appeal for the gang.

Debbie was a notable exception; she had lost a great deal of weight since she had retired, due to a combination of intense exercise and a membership in Weight Watchers. She had even checked out potential Weight Watchers meetings along our route, but she realized that attending any would slow us down way too much.

We left Jean and were back on the road at about ten thirty, and everybody was already tired. I think the adrenaline was wearing off, and the grind was setting in.

We started e-mailing back and forth to decide if we should stick to our plan of driving through the night or stop and get some sleep. We delayed a decision, but I had a feeling that sleep was going to win out, and it probably should have. The downside to traveling when exhausted outweighed the upside of sticking to our schedule, which had been arbitrarily created.

Pretty soon I found myself experiencing a first; I was seeing Vegas without stopping there. The skyline was off in the distance, like a mirage. I imagined that it was the first time that a mirage actually contained a hotel named after itself. I'd have given anything to march into that Mirage or the Wynn or the Mandalay Bay Hotel & Casino with Wanda the mastiff on my arm. But, alas, it was not to be.

We pulled over into a large field behind a Love's rest stop just an hour past Vegas, set up the fencing, and unloaded the dogs again. It was only the second time we'd done it, but I was already pretty sick of it. Everybody else seemed to be in a permanent state of good cheer, and fortunately we were able to do it a little faster that time, probably because we were more familiar with the process.

A bunch of people went into Love's to once again load up on junk food, and they reported that there were showers in there that we could rent in the morning. That was good to hear, because while there were showers on the RVs, they were small and it seemed inconceivable that anyone would use them. It would entail a risk of running out of water, and the way the vehicles shook, it would also present the possibility of being thrown naked and wet into the main cabin. I for one had little desire to see a naked, soaking Emmit flopping around the RV.

It was of course very dark, especially since the sky seemed cloudy, and I was worried about dogs getting away through the fence, unseen. But once we got them back on, we did another rigorous check, and everyone was accounted for.

There was a unanimity of feeling that we should stay there and get a few hours sleep, and I was certainly fine with that. It was becoming obvious to me that we were not going to make it on our schedule, but I hadn't had much confidence in that schedule anyway. I'd wait a day or so to get a better idea, and then call ahead to advise the bed-and-breakfast waiting for the team on the other end.

So we all found beds and couches in the vehicles, most already occupied by dogs, and settled in for at least part of the night. It was a little after one in the morning, and I set my alarm for five o'clock, at which point I'd get everyone up. At home the dogs usually wake us at five thirty, but there was no telling what they'd do in this situation.

On my RV, Erik and Nick decided to go for a walk before going to sleep, and they left as Emmit and I were dozing off.

And then the sky exploded.

Benji

I was at our vet in Orange County for what seemed like a daily visit when the office manager, Julie, approached me. She told me that a dog had been abandoned there by an owner who no longer wanted him. The dog was a four-year-old Bernese mountain dog named Benji, and since she knew how much Debbie and I loved that breed, she was wondering if we would be interested in taking him.

She confided in me that while he had been there six weeks, the vet who owned the place, Dr. Kali, had instructed her not to tell me about him. He didn't want to take advantage of us or make us feel obligated. She finally couldn't take it anymore and told me.

I went into the back to see Benji, who was about as far from a Bernese mountain dog as it's possible to be. I have no idea what he is—probably a mixture of shepherd, Lab, and Rottweiler—but he is absolutely beautiful.

He was lying in a dog run, actually more like cowering, when I went in to see him. I leaned over to pet him, and he urinated all over the floor and himself. This was one scared dog.

I went back out to the reception area, where Julie was waiting. She was also laughing. She had lied about the Bernese mountain dog part, as I had already discovered, because she knew that once I saw Benji I would not be able to refuse him. Within fifteen minutes he was in my car, not an easy trick to manage, because he was so fearful.

I would say it took forty-eight hours for Benji to become a completely new dog. He absolutely loved our house and bonded with a shepherd mix named Otis. They are both on the young side for our group, so they are energetic wrestlers with each other. If Benji goes to the groomer's, Otis cries until he comes home.

Benji remained slightly skittish for a couple of months, but now he is as affectionate, loving, and all-around terrific as a dog can be. He has adjusted extraordinarily well to Maine, and he loves running in the woods in the snow.

I talked to him recently about the strides he's made since that day at the vet's office, but he pretended not to have any recollection of it.

Wanda

As I mentioned before, one of my favorite places to do book signings is Houston. The local golden rescue group is the gold standard, and the local mystery bookstore, Murder By The Book, is absolutely terrific. They always combine to put on a great event when I'm there.

When I'm traveling on tour, I can't help but feel a little guilty about leaving Debbie at home to take care of the dogs by herself. Feeding them, cleaning up, petting them, going to the vet . . . it is definitely a minimum-two-person job.

I check in with her repeatedly, so frequently that it drives her crazy, and I ask her to call me if there are any problems. There is never anything she can't handle, but I still want to know what's going on.

On this particular trip to Houston, I was leaving the hotel to drive to the event when I got an ominous e-mail from her. The East Valley shelter had called; there was a ten-year-old golden that was going to be put down that afternoon if Debbie didn't come and get it.

On its face that was no problem. We were always talking about cutting back on the number of dogs in our house, but we never seemed to follow through on it. And we were not about to say no to a senior golden.

The reason it was so frightening was that Debbie was going to a shelter.

A bad shelter.

By herself, without me to rein her in.

In my mind's eye I could see her walking through the shelter, pointing to the dogs, saying, "I'll take you and you and you and you . . . aw, what the heck, you too."

I had just arrived at the event when I got the next e-mail. The golden, she said, was terribly matted but beautiful. She was also already spayed, which meant that Debbie would be able to take her right away and bring her to our vet to get checked out and bathed. Debbie had named her Mamie.

She went on to say that there was an eleven-year-old border collie mix "to die for." She didn't say that she was taking this second dog, but I figured there was approximately a 100 percent chance that she would. Or maybe a little higher.

The next e-mail came ten minutes later. There was a twelve-year-old Lab mix who looked "just like Waldo." Waldo was a black Lab that had died a short time before. He was a great dog whose most distinguishing trait was a snore that could be heard for miles. Again, no mention of whether she was taking this other dog, but no doubt either.

"We really don't need any more dogs," I wrote back, and her reply was "I completely agree. Just these three."

I was about to start my speech when I got what would be

the last e-mail of the afternoon. It was short and to the point. "There is a 105-pound, emaciated mastiff that is amazing. I've named her Wanda."

Debbie didn't say that she was taking her, but it was fairly hard to picture her leaving behind an "emaciated, amazing" dog, especially since we had always wanted a mastiff. And it would have been downright silly to name a dog that was staying in the shelter.

So it was that Wanda and all the rest joined our little group. If Debbie felt any embarrassment or regret about gorging herself on rescue dogs, she hid it well. Her reason for taking Wanda, she explained when we spoke on the phone later, was that not to do so would have resulted in Wanda's being put down or perhaps taken by someone who would keep her outside all day.

She said that Wanda had gotten up on her hind legs and hugged Debbie with her front paws through the cage bars. That, she explained, had clinched the sale, though I've got a hunch the sale was clinched the moment Debbie set eyes on her.

We took Wanda to our vet, as we did with all newcomers. He checked her out and the staff gave her a bath, and then began picking the ticks off of her. They counted over four hundred of them, which disgustingly revealed how mistreated she had been. Even worse, Wanda truly was terribly undernourished. I could see every one of her ribs; I will never understand how someone could fail to provide food for a dog. But that wasn't going to be a problem at our house.

Once we got her home, Wanda gained weight so fast that I think Debbie must have been slipping her bowling-ball-sized biscuits. I assume her ribs are still there, but they soon retreated from sight, and Wanda currently weighs 165 pounds.

There are only four dogs currently capable of getting up

onto our bed without assistance. Three of them—Jenny, Benji, and Otis—are relatively young and can jump high enough to get there. The fourth, Wanda, would never dream of jumping. She simply steps onto the bed, as if it were a curb.

Amazingly, she doesn't seem to take up that much room on the bed. She finds her spot in the crowd and sort of curls up. She's comforting to sleep next to; we call her the Great Wall of Wanda. She snores loudly, and for a few months Debbie thought it was me. Then one day I was out of town and the snoring continued, which got me off the hook.

Our bed is truly something to see at night. There are always four or five dogs up there, including Wanda and Bernie, the Bernese mountain dog. Everybody prefers Debbie to me, so they all get as close to her as they can, leaving me relatively unimpeded.

In Santa Monica, Debbie's side of the bed was about two feet from the window, and I walked in one night to find her asleep, but so crowded that her feet were on the windowsill.

And the noises in our bedroom are unbelievable. Between the snoring and the scratching, the collars jiggling, and all the other weird noises, it sounds like a jungle in Zaire.

But back to Wanda. When it came to feeding time, she was hilarious. She got the same amount of food as the others, the only difference being that she viewed the serving as the appetizer. Once she was finished, usually about fifteen seconds after she started, she went on patrol.

She knew which dogs were unlikely to finish their meals, and she was on the scene when they walked away from their dish. She then inhaled what they'd left behind and moved on to the next one.

Wanda is a serious eater.

She is also a gentle giant, obedient and wanting only to be petted. She craves human contact. It is scary to think how many Wandas are out there, being used as guard dogs or stuck outside in deference to their size.

Wanda belongs in the house, on the bed, on the couch, wherever the hell she wants to go. And that is how she is going to spend the rest of her life.

Otis

Lorie Armbruster, a friend and terrific rescue person in Orange County, called with a problem. Their rescue group had a three-year-old shepherd mix named Otis that they had unsuccessfully placed three times. Each time, he had been returned with a complaint; he was too aloof or too aggressive or too skittish or too whatever.

They felt that he might be unadoptable, and euthanasia was under consideration. That was why she turned to us, even though Otis was a much younger dog than we usually took in.

When I went to get Otis, Lorie gave me a speech about his emotional issues, one of which was that he was completely unfriendly, bordering on aggressive, with women. Perhaps a woman had mistreated him earlier in his life, but there was no way to know that now.

I brought Otis home, and it was clear that he loved having the other dogs around. Debbie was at work, so I called her and told her that she should be very careful around Otis until we learned whether or not he presented a danger.

When she came home, she sat on the couch quietly with a glass of wine. It was hard for her to drink it, though, because Otis jumped up on the couch, draped himself across her lap, and went to sleep. I told Debbie that she must not be a real woman.

Otis has a bunch of friends that he wrestles and runs in the Maine woods with. His best friend is Benji; they are completely inseparable.

Simon the Psycho

A couple of years ago we got a call from a rescue group alerting us to a very difficult situation. A family in the San Fernando Valley had a ten-year-old golden mix named Simon. He had been theirs since he was a puppy, and they loved him and provided a good home for him.

Then one day, for no apparent reason, he bit the woman, inflicting a small but significant amount of damage. They had two young children, and they instantly and correctly decided that they couldn't keep Simon and risk injury to those children.

But they overreacted. Rather than moving cautiously, they brought Simon to the East Valley shelter and turned him in. Not wanting to entirely abandon him to the system, they notified rescue groups and asked them to intervene if Simon didn't get adopted through the shelter.

Unfortunately, the system isn't set up to work that way.

Since they reported the bite and the woman got medical care for it, the shelter was not allowed legally to adopt Simon out to anyone other than a registered rescue group.

The normal procedure in situations like this is for them to hold on to a dog for ten days to make sure it doesn't have rabies. Then, after that period and if a rescue group hadn't put in a claim for it, it would be put down.

So Simon's only chance was a rescue group, but that was a slim one. Simon was a mix and therefore didn't qualify for breed rescues. The few groups that take mixes are generally overcrowded, and with all the great dogs in the system, why would they use a space on a senior who bites? For obvious reasons, he would be extraordinarily hard for them to place.

So we took Simon. He was adorable and friendly, and exhibited no aggressive tendencies whatsoever. That's not to say he didn't have his idiosyncrasies. For instance, he went crazy whenever he was on the other side of a closed door from Bernie, the Bernese mountain dog. We would put Bernie into a room by himself to eat, to prevent him from taking everybody else's food. Simon would bark like a lunatic outside the door until Bernie came out, and then he was fine again.

Simon seemed to like me more than he did Debbie, and he followed me around all day. This made him quite unusual; almost every dog we ever had preferred Debbie, and we've had a lot of them. His favorite spot was on the chair in my office, where he stayed while I was working on my computer.

He was in that position one day when Debbie came into the office. She went over to Simon to pet him. He was looking right at her, so he wasn't taken by surprise . . . but she was. He bit her on the arm and hand. The wounds required twelve stitches.

I reluctantly came to the conclusion that we needed to put him down; we simply couldn't keep such an obvious danger to life and limb. I contacted his previous family, who had occasionally been coming to visit him. They didn't resist; as much as they loved Simon, they agreed that we needed to do what we needed to do.

The only one who didn't agree was Debbie. Simon has this sweet, friendly way about him (when he isn't ripping humans apart), and she couldn't bear to kill him. We'd just have to be more careful.

And we have been. As of this writing, it's been two years since Simon bit Debbie, and there hasn't been another incident. This is a surprise, since by other standards he's even nuttier than he used to be.

For instance, in the Maine house there's a staircase to the second floor that has a railing alongside it. Whenever there's any kind of barking, Simon runs up the stairs, and Bernie runs to the side of the railing on the first floor. They then bark furiously and angrily at each other, venting their outrage while secure in the knowledge that the railing is protecting them both.

But it is amazing how few times we've been bitten by any of our dogs. The worst bite I suffered was from a collie mix named Sadie, a crotchety old lady who was one of the first dogs we ever took into our home. Sadie considered herself royalty, and she did not suffer fools easily.

She didn't like anything about me, and she made that quite clear one day when she bit me on the elbow. And she didn't just bite me; she dug her teeth in to the point that when I lifted my arm in pain, she hung on, and I raised her off the ground.

Even with all that, the damage wasn't particularly severe, and I didn't even go to the doctor. That presented something of a problem, since it left me with no credible way of garnering sympathy from Debbie.

She was coming in from a business trip that night, and I went to pick her up at the airport. I wasn't in that much pain, but I decided that a sling would be the best way to demonstrate the trauma and suffering I had experienced. So I created a makeshift one and wore it.

It was, of course, the first thing that Debbie noticed, and she asked what had happened, her voice reflecting real concern.

"Sadie bit me," I said. "And she dug her teeth in so hard that I lifted her off the ground."

"What did you do to her?"

"Nothing yet," I said, hoping to be praised for my restraint.

"No, I meant what did you do to make her bite you?"

So there it was . . . out in the open. Debbie was taking Sadie's side against me. She was siding with the predator over the victim.

I would like to say it was an isolated incident, but alas, this book is nonfiction. In Debbie's view, dogs can do no wrong.

If a dog takes something off my desk and chews it, her view is I left it too close to the edge.

One of them pissed on the floor? Must be a bladder infection.

Barking too loudly and too often? They must have seen an animal outside.

Simon bites her and gives her twelve stitches? She startled him and he was reacting in understandable self-defense.

Suffice it to say that when I screw up, I don't get that much consideration and understanding.

Not even when I'm wearing a sling.

Kaboom

I think the first thing I sensed was that Otis was pacing. Otis is a ninety-pound shepherd mix, and I didn't notice him because he was making noise; I noticed him because the pacing he was doing was on my chest.

Even if he had been making a racket, I wouldn't have heard it, because within moments the thunder was so loud that no other sound could possibly intrude upon it. And then there were also the flashes of lightning, which turned the area into daylight every four or five seconds. Looking out the window was like watching the "shock and awe" attacks on Baghdad on CNN, minus Bernie Shaw's reporting.

Keep in mind that our dogs are from Southern California, so they basically had no idea what thunder and lightning were. I myself hadn't been in a thunderstorm for almost twenty years, and probably had never been in one that severe in my life. I certainly had never been in one in Vegas, because it almost never rains in the casinos.

The ironic thing is that lack of weather, and especially thunderstorms, had been one of my expressed reasons for wanting to leave California and head east. I love thunderstorms and always have; I have fond memories from growing up of sitting on our front porch in Paterson, New Jersey, and watching the pounding rain bouncing off the road. But this one was not particularly well-timed.

The noise coming from the outside was deafening, and trying to sleep was impossible; I finally knew what it must be like to be our neighbor. During the brief pauses when the thunder stopped, I could tell that our dogs were barking, though in comparison to the crashing thunder, they sounded like Simon and Garfunkel singing "Sounds of Silence."

Actually, they were not going as nuts as I would have expected. Otis continued to pace, and I'd moved him to the floor. Simon also seemed agitated, though he hadn't bitten anyone, and Benji was at the window, trying to figure out what the hell could possibly be going on.

I hadn't moved from the bench I was lying on, and it was going to take a lot more than a storm to budge me. I was actually fairly comfortable, and my sense was that I was not going to have very many moments like that on the trip.

Emmit had obviously been wakened by the storm, and he yelled out to me that Erik and Nick hadn't come back. He had last seen them lying out on the grass, apparently preferring to sleep under the sky, unencumbered by dogs. But that was obviously prior to the storm.

I was worried about them, and I assessed my options. I could stay where I was, comfortable and under a blanket, and do *nothing. Or I could go outside in that ridiculous storm and try to find them.*

It was the definition of a no-brainer.

I've had much tougher rationalizations, since there were only two realistic possibilities. Erik and Nick were not banging on the door to be let in, so they'd either found cover or been hit by lightning. If they'd found cover, they were fine. If they'd been hit by lightning, they were dead. Either way, there was really nothing for me to do.

The odds against the third possibility, that they had been hit by lightning and survived, were minuscule. As they say, there's more chance of getting hit by lightning than that happening. And it's not like I'd been trained in anti-lightning CPR; what the hell would I do if I found them? I think I read somewhere that the best thing to do with a lightning victim is let them sleep it off in the rain.

Besides, selfless as I am, I had to consider the repercussions should something happen to me. The dogs needed me on the vehicle. What if I were to go outside and get hit by lightning myself? Who would be the trip leader? What would happen to the dogs that love me so? I needed to survive for the greater good.

Obviously, I had no role to play in this crisis.

Debbie called to ask if we were OK, and I told her that we were fine, and that the dogs were doing well. She said that her gang was surprisingly calm, and she was going to call the other RV and check in on them.

When I made the mistake of telling her that Erik and Nick were outside, she said, "Shouldn't you make sure they're OK?"

"I'm sure they're fine," I said.

"In this storm?"

"It's not really that bad; it sounds a lot worse than it is."

And then, as if on cue, the RV door opened and Erik and Nick came in, soaking wet but otherwise intact. Of course, Debbie wasn't aware of that, so I said, "I've got to go look for them. I don't care about the personal danger; I'm responsible for the members of this team."

When I hung up I said, "Welcome back," to Erik and Nick. "You guys OK?"

"It's raining like crazy out there," Erik said.

"Really? I hadn't noticed."

The storm went on for at least another half hour. I thought we were parked on a dirt lot, and my fear was that we were going to wake up and find ourselves bumper-deep in mud. It wasn't a strong enough fear to get me to go outside and check; no fear could be that strong.

Of course, whatever the terrain was like, we were going to have to walk the dogs on it, so if it was muddy, that could be very unpleasant. There were no hoses to wash them off, and not enough water if there had been hoses.

Eventually my alarm went off, and after five minutes of gearing myself up, I set out to wake everybody. The dogs were slow to rise, but the humans seemed eager and alert and raring to go.

The ground wasn't bad at all; I guess the area must have needed the rain. We set up our mini dog park and let the gang out. We were getting better at it; everybody seemed to know their assignments, and it all just kicked into gear.

Most people reported getting some sleep, which was fairly amazing under the circumstances. Everybody had a story to tell, mostly about the experience of waking up with dogs in their faces. Cyndi Flores was crowded to the point that she'd slept on a bench with her feet up on the cooler containing the meatballs.

It was our first feeding time, so I took a large bag out of the storage area and put food into twenty-five dishes. At home we al-ways put some wet food on top of the dry to make it more tasty and palatable, but I'd decided not to do it on this trip. It would take time and involve too many hassles: washing the dishes, opening the cans, et cetera. I am a master at hassle avoidance.

The dogs barely ate, except of course for Wanda, which was no great surprise. They'd been under considerable stress, with their new surroundings and new human companions, and stress will often make them less likely to eat. We see it when we bring a new dog into our house; in some cases it can take twenty-four hours before they're chomping down.

I was sure we were well behind schedule, but I really had no way to accurately judge that. We were going to have to figure it out soon, since we had the hotel reserved in Maine and, more sig-nificant, people had flights home. We were supposed to get there on that coming Thursday, and the flights were on Friday. I didn't think we were going to make it.

We got some bad news when we learned that the Love's rest stop had lost its electric power in the storm, so the showers wouldn't be available. It wasn't such a disaster that day, since we had all showered the day before. But if things like that kept happening, it could get quite unpleasant.

The same drivers—Emmit, Randy, and Joe—were behind the wheel when we left. They'd been the only drivers so far, and they seemed fine with it. I assumed they had taken a look at the rest of us and decided that they would rather drive in a state of exhaus-tion than risk dying with us.

Joe reported that Wanda the mastiff insisted on climbing onto the driver's seat with him. He resisted my offer to move her onto my RV. Joe and Terri were totally pleasant, go-with-the-flow-type people; in fact, the entire group seemed to fit into that category.

The first stop was for gas; by then our gas bill was approximately the GDP of Uruguay. We'd been using Debbie's credit card, and twice the company cut off credit, thinking that somebody must have stolen the card and was using it fraudulently. Each time she had to call them and explain the situation, and then deal with the laughter and surprise of the person at the credit card company.

One less-than-swift representative whom Debbie told we were traveling from California to Maine thought that meant we were traveling internationally, and tried to switch the call to that department.

Of course, every time we stopped, the dogs wanted to get off the vehicles. The driving motion lulled them, but when we stopped they decided to head for the exits. This time we didn't let them off, since they had just been walked and it would mean an extra forty-five minutes to do so. Benji in particular was annoyed by the decision and loudly barked his disapproval.

That set the rest of them off barking, and the other customers in the gas station looked in the windows to see what was going on. Strangers peering in at them made the dogs even nuttier, and the barking got that much louder, attracting more people. And so on and so on and so on . . .

My hope was that none of these people worked for local animal control. In fact, my fear was that somebody was going to think we were abusing the dogs or illegally transporting them and call an animal control officer. So we took the time to patiently explain to people what was going on, and most of them seemed to buy our story.

I wished they would have bought our gas instead.

Big Sarah

We have rescued thousands of dogs from many different places, but only one from a pet store . . . Sarah, the Bernese mountain dog.

I say this with some embarrassment, because in my view, getting one dog from a pet store is one too many. Doing so encourages the proliferation and continued operation of puppy mills, which no dog lover should want to do. Having said that, I have never regretted for a minute that we got Sarah.

Debbie had been shopping with a friend in a mall, and the friend needed to buy something in the pet store. Debbie went in with her, only to discover that it was a store that sold puppies. And one particular puppy caught her eye: a Bernese that, according to the information on the cage, was five months old.

She was not the most beautiful of Berneses, not even close, and she had been in the store, in the same cage, for more than two months. And that cage was by that point way too small for her; she had almost no room to stand up or turn around.

That was not a situation that was likely to change any time soon. The adjacent cages all had much smaller, much younger, and much cuter puppies. It seemed extraordinarily unlikely that someone was going to come in and choose Sarah; that isn't how people buy puppies.

Debbie had a conversation with the storeowner, who confirmed that pessimistic view. She was preparing to send Sarah back to the breeder to get her money back, which would have left Sarah to an uncertain, probably grim, fate.

So Debbie negotiated a price that reflected the circumstances and could in no way be seen as an inducement for the store to keep selling puppies. She brought Sarah home, and since then, if there has ever been a day or a moment that Sarah wasn't smiling, I must have missed it.

She's now nine years old, which is a very advanced age for a Berner, and she's still as active as a puppy. She is also the house barking instigator; no matter what the catalyst, she is the first one to see it and bark at it, and the others follow suit.

Sarah has very serious arthritis, and two tumors that are inoperable and will ultimately do her in. But for the time being, she seems happy every day and loves life, and that's what it's about for us.

The Barking. My God, the Barking

Since most of our dogs are old, they sleep the majority of the day. I've often said that the inside of our house seems like a Civil War battlefield when the fighting was over and the guns had stopped firing . . . eerily quiet, with bodies lying everywhere.

But if FedEx shows up or the gardener is outside, the dogs spring into action, and it sounds like a foxhunt has broken out.

Things that normal people think nothing of cause us to cringe. For instance, Domino's commercials invariably begin with a shot of the deliveryman ringing a doorbell. It may be a thirty-second spot, but the effect of that doorbell lasts a lot longer than thirty seconds. I can be in New York at a hotel, and if I see one of those commercials come on the television, I instinctively and involuntarily brace myself for an audio onslaught.

The noise of a barking explosion can be absolutely deafening, and it always comes at an inopportune time. It usually starts with an outburst at five thirty in the morning, telling us that the dogs have decided it is time to get up. And while daylight savings time might provide other people with an extra hour of sleep on the night the clocks are changed, not us. The dogs operate on their own body clock.

When she was working, Debbie would make business phone calls to New York starting at six A.M. California time. A planned five-minute call could take three times that long, allowing for long periods of barking to block out all communications.

The people on the New York end apparently thought it was hilarious, and they would regale us with stories about how they put the calls on the speakerphone, and everybody gathered around to hear the insanity and laugh.

We never found it quite so funny.

I frequently have occasion to do live radio interviews about my books with stations around the country. I can count the number of times that the dogs didn't bark during those interviews on very few fingers.

One time I was doing an interview with a Baltimore station, and I began, as I often do, by alerting the host and apologizing in advance for the fact that there might be a barking outburst in the middle of the interview.

The session was nearing an end, and amazingly there had not been a peep. Apparently, whichever dog was in charge of alerting the others that there was an interview to ruin had fallen asleep on the job. So before we signed off, the host rather smugly pointed out that my concern had been unwarranted, that there wasn't a dog to be heard. He even jokingly asked if I had been telling the truth about our living situation.

I asked him to hold on for a few seconds, and I walked to the front door and opened it. I reached around and rang the doorbell, and the place absolutely exploded in a crescendo of noise. I held the phone to the sound for a few moments, and then yelled into the phone, "WHAT DO YOU THINK NOW?" before hanging up.

At the first sign of barking during those interviews, I would hide in a room with the doors closed. They haven't invented doors that could keep out the kinds of sounds our dogs could generate, but they helped a little.

One time I was doing an interview with a Seattle station, and I was hiding in a closed room to avoid the noise. I wasn't having much success, so I further insulated myself by going into a closet within that room and closing that door as well. So there I was, sitting in a dark closet at night, talking to a Seattle radio host. I felt like Tom Hanks.

I told the host what I was doing, and he laughed at the mere thought of my hiding like that. I told him that when the barking died down, he would soon be able to publicize the fact that an author had come out of the closet, live on his show.

But when we lived in Santa Monica, the absolute worst day of the year, every year, was Halloween. We lived in a neighborhood with a lot of families with little kids.

Kids who went trick-or-treating.

Kids who rang doorbells.

So we would block off the back half of the house, and Debbie would take all the dogs back there with her. I would then open the front door and plant a chair in the doorway, where I would sit with a bag of whatever treat it was we were giving out.

This had a double effect. First, it prevented the little monsters from ringing the doorbell, and second, it made me look like an idiot.

It was a small price to pay.

So to sum up, having all these dogs has made me a happy, loving person, except for the things that I hate.

Like television commercials.

And FedEx drivers.

And gardeners.

And mail carriers.

And little kids.

And workmen.

And fireworks.

And visitors.

And other neighborhood animals.

And thunder.

And doorbells.

Doorbells are the worst.

Noel and Kahlani

Noel and Kahlani are goldens that we got within a week of each other. Kahlani already had a name that the shelter knew, but Noel didn't. Since we got her a week before Christmas, Debbie named her Noel. If we had gotten her a week before Hanukkah, she might be named Moishe.

Noel and Kahlani are similar in terms of looks and demeanor. Both are light-colored and smallish, though Noel is the smaller of the two. Kahlani could stand to lose some weight; it seems she and I must have the same personal trainer.

Kahlani has recently discovered a new place to sleep, in the recliner chair that one would think would be reserved for humans. She's even learned that by resting her body against the back of it, she can get it to recline, giving her considerably more room to sleep.

Noel likes to hang out in either my office closet or a small area behind my desk. She's adorable and wouldn't harm a fly, but it's fair to say that house-training is not her specialty.

Both of them, like all the other dogs in our house, are safe and loved. And that's really all we can do, all we concentrate on. How they choose to spend their time is their business, and we don't try to influence them. If they want to stay apart from the other dogs and sleep the days away, good for them. If they want to wrestle and run around, also fine.

All our dogs have had enough stress in their lives. Once we get them, it's smooth sailing.

Woofabago

I checked my BlackBerry and discovered that I had 114 e-mails that I hadn't yet read. Since I have a total of about four friends, and even they're not particularly crazy about me, this was slightly unusual. The only time I get a boatload of e-mails is when a book has just come out and readers are responding to my request for feedback. But I hadn't had a new book out for a couple of months.

I started to read the messages and found that most were from readers telling me that they were following our adventure on "Woofabago" on Facebook. And based on the Facebook posts, it sounded like everybody, the people on the trip and the ones following it, were having a blast.

I partially understood it. If I were at home, watching football, drinking a beer, and occasionally checking out Facebook, I'd be having a hell of a time as well. The best part would be reminding myself that I was at home and not on an RV riding cross-country with twenty-five dogs.

A typical post from our group was made on the first morning. It said, "Yay! We have over 500 'Likes' . . . a 25-wagging-tail salute to you all from all of us here on the Woofabago adventure. Consider yourselves honorary members of our Merry Band of Lunatics!"

Ugh.

Worst of all, Facebook was filled with pictures of the trip, including many of me. I had this image of social media exploding with talk of the fat, gray-haired lunatic with all the dogs. Had I known the pictures were being taken, I wouldn't have exhaled.

At the next stop, I asked around and found out that the person running our Facebook operation was Cindy Spodek Dickey. That made sense; she's an executive in the tech industry, and in fact was working at Microsoft when she met Debbie. Together they did a highly successful Taco Bell/Xbox promotion.

Cindy is a very upbeat person, which makes her my natural opposite. She's also completely at home in social media land, while I'm only completely at home when I'm at home.

But she was not identifying herself by name in her posts, and since I was the figurehead of the operation, people were just naturally assuming that I was the one writing them. These were clearly people who didn't know me; if they had, they'd have known that posts that did not include whining and complaining could not be mine.

And the only way I would use the words "wagging-tail salute" would be if an upbeat pod had taken over my body.

But I was getting credit for writing the posts, so I hurried to disabuse everyone of that notion with my actual first Facebook post. I credited Cindy for her work keeping America informed, and made sure that everyone knew I hadn't been involved. I didn't want anyone to think I was having fun; it would be too confusing when I killed myself midway across the country.

"What a shame," they would say. "And he seemed to be enjoying himself so much."

But I couldn't worry about that right then; it was finally time to change drivers. Emmit, Joe, and Randy had been handling the chores exclusively, and they needed a break, even if they wouldn't admit it. So I told Emmit that I was taking the wheel at the next gas stop, and I did so.

As we were about to leave, Emmit got back in the RV and sat in the passenger seat. He told me that Debbie and Cyndi were taking the wheel in the RVs that would be following us. In deference to the fact that it was their first time driving this kind of vehicle, we needed to take it slow and careful.

He said that I should keep my speed to no higher than fifty miles per hour and should stay in the right-hand lane. It was a good twenty miles an hour slower than we had been traveling, but Emmit said that later, when Debbie and Cyndi were more used to it, we could speed up.

So I did what Emmit said, even though it felt like we were crawling along. At that pace, we'd be in Maine in time to watch the Super Bowl.

When we got to the next dog-walking stop, Debbie came up to me and asked, "What is going on?"

"What do you mean?"

"Are you driving with the emergency brake on?"

"Emmit felt that with you and Cyndi driving for the first time, we should take it easy," I said.

She nodded. "That would make some sense—not much, but some—if Cyndi and I were driving. But it's still been Joe and Randy."

I reported this piece of news to Emmit, and it turned out that *he hadn't been completely truthful with me. Another way to put it would be that he lied through his teeth.*

Apparently, Emmit has a well-developed instinct for self-preservation, and he made the assessment that his life would be imperiled if I was to drive an RV at a high speed with him in it. It's a point of view that did have some logic to it.

But I took the wheel again, this time with Debbie and Cyndi actually doing the same. What I hadn't realized was that we were about to be driving across the Rockies, which meant a lot of turns and bends in the road, and some moments when we seemed a little close to elevated edges. There were also hills; it turned out the Rockies have a lot of them.

It was a little scary, especially since it was nighttime, but nothing too daunting. If it weren't for the fact that I was driving this strange, enormous vehicle, I wouldn't have thought anything of it.

Debbie had a different point of view, and in the time since, to hear her describe it, you would think that we were hanging by our fingertips from a high cliff while being attacked by Geronimo and his warriors.

But the twists and turns made me go close to the speed Emmit had advised, so he seemed somewhat satisfied. I wouldn't say he was completely comfortable, because about every thirty or forty seconds he asked me if I wanted him to take over.

We stopped for a late dinner, which Mary Lynn's son had prepared in advance. It was spaghetti and meatballs, and Mary Lynn and Cyndi heated it while the dogs were wandering around the fenced-in area we'd set up for what seemed like the hundredth time.

You've never lived until you've eaten spaghetti and meatballs off paper plates, standing in an area pretty much covered in dog shit. Of course, it was almost completely dark out, so there was no way to actually see the dog shit, which made stepping an adventure, and something to be avoided.

The food was actually delicious, and it was a nice change. For me, it was a change from the cold cuts and fruit I had bought; for everyone else it was a change from the convenience-store stuff they'd been inhaling. Based on how my food had gone over with everyone, you'd think I'd sprayed it with pesticide before we left.

Everybody was getting tired, a combination of the arduousness of the trip and the fact that no one had gotten much real sleep during the Vegas deluge. Not too many people seemed to be able to nap while we were driving, probably due to a combination of being thrown around by the rattling vehicles and having dogs licking their faces.

So we agreed to think about whether and where we were going to stop for the night, and we'd make the decision at our next gas station visit.

Based on the way the vehicles sucked up fuel, I figured that would be in about four minutes.

Frank

I was giving a talk at the Poisoned Pen Bookstore in Phoenix, which I do pretty much every time a new book of mine comes out, when in strode Frank. Thus ended my time as the focal point of the room.

I wasn't surprised to see him; the rescue group had told me they were bringing him. We had already arranged that I would take him home, and I was therefore going to drive, rather than fly, back to California.

He was exactly as they described—frail, old, white in the face—and he walked as if he were pulling a wagon. He was perfect, and as he was led toward the front of the room, he had to run a gauntlet of hands from people trying to pet him.

The rescue people had actually led me to believe that he was in worse physical condition than turned out to be the case. Once we got him on pain meds for his arthritis and put him on a special diet for his stomach issues, he was basically fine.

There was nothing extraordinary about Frank's time with us. He was an affectionate, loving golden retriever that never gave us a moment's trouble. He was slowing down considerably by the time we started on our trip, but he made it with flying colors.

Frank died about six months after we got to Maine. I can certainly report that his last years were contented ones.

My Career Went to the Dogs

My movie marketing career had very little to do with animals, dogs or otherwise. I did some work on the advertising for the *Benji* movies, but nothing of consequence.

Very early in my career, I was with an ad agency involved with the advertising for MGM's Saturday matinee re-release of *The Yearling*. My client had, it's fair to say, a rather bizarre devotion to the series of family films that MGM was running as matinees, and *The Yearling* was the first.

The ad that we were working with was a shot of the boy carrying the fawn, but it was larger than we had space for. My solution to making the ad smaller, I proudly announced, was to "crop the dog," thereby not showing the animal's entire body. Suffice it to say that the client was not too pleased that I thought the fawn in his precious movie was a dog.

The only other connection to anything with animals in my marketing career was on a film called *The Bear*. It was a pickup for our company, which meant that it was produced independently, and then we bought it for distribution.

The Bear was an interesting movie made by a talented director named Jean-Jacques Annaud. Two bears were on the screen for virtually the entire movie, and as I recall, the only humans were two hunters, who were shown only briefly and who spoke almost no dialogue.

Six executives, including me, flew to Paris on the Concorde to get our first look at the movie we had bought. We huddled in a small room with Mr. Annaud, and he presented a three-hour version of the film on a Moviola. For those too young to know what that was, it was a machine that ran the film and had a very small screen on which it could be watched. Directors used it to experiment, splicing film together in the editing process. Very, very pre-digital.

So there we were in a small room in Paris, standing in front of this little machine, when Annaud announced that the sound was not ready, so we would be watching the film without sound. But not to worry, he said, because since most of the sound in the final film would be bear noises, he would stand next to the Moviola and mimic bear sounds himself, to give us a flavor of what the finished product would be like.

So for three hours we watched footage on this little screen in Paris, with a Frenchman making bear noises. I remember looking at Jeff Sagansky, the president of production for our company, and I knew that he was thinking, as I was, how surreal and ridiculous the situation was.

Three months later, we had a screening of a rough cut of the movie in Paramus, New Jersey. We had invited an audience in, and as was standard procedure, we would hand them comment cards, soliciting their opinions when the film was concluded.

Jeff and I were standing in the back of the theater when two things of note happened. First, we both realized that the bear noises were exactly the same as in Paris. To this day I believe that every bear noise in the finished film actually consists of the director mimicking bear noises. He would deny it, and I certainly could never prove it, but I think it's true.

Second, a woman stormed out of her seat and walked out. She saw Jeff and me as she was leaving, and somehow she knew that we were executives with the company that owned the movie.

There had been a brief scene that showed one bear humping the other, probably because that's what bears do. But she was outraged, claiming that she was told that the film was appropriate for family viewing. Yet in her eyes it was nothing more than bear porno! With full frontal bear nudity!

It was a weird night at the movies.

It wasn't until I was writing TV movies that I was turning into a real-life dog lunatic, and I decided to put a golden retriever in one of my movies. It was called *Deadly Isolation*, and was the story of a woman who lived with her senior golden on the coast of Maine.

There is no reason to bore you with all the details of the plot. I'll just say that a man comes to the house, pretending to be something and someone he is not. His goal, in order to pull off a nefarious scheme, includes getting the woman to fall for him.

One scene in the script had the woman, the bad guy, and the golden go out on the ocean in her boat. When she is not looking, he throws the dog into the water. Then he jumps in to heroically save the dog, earning the woman's gratitude and adoration in the process.

Brilliant stuff.

Unfortunately, the film was a very low-budget production, and there was apparently not enough money to have the scene shot out on the ocean. So instead they shot it in what was little more than a viaduct, about as wide as a half-dozen bowling alleys.

For some reason, they used a Bernese mountain dog instead of a golden, which was fine. But when the guy throws the dog into the placid body of water, the dog starts swimming happily along, and it's all the guy can do to catch up to it.

Not my finest creative moment.

When I started writing Andy Carpenter novels, I gave Andy a dog named Tara. (Where would I have gotten that name?) Andy is also into dog rescue and runs the Tara Foundation. As you can probably tell, this was not exactly a huge stretch for me.

And the books were doing reasonably well. People seemed to like them, and they got a bunch of award nominations. *Bury the Lead* was even chosen by Janet Evanovich as a *Today Show* Book of the Month, and we went on the show together, where Janet was incredibly complimentary and gracious.

I had decided that I wanted to try other things, and since the books were selling only moderately well, the sixth in the series, *Play Dead*, was going to be the last one.

That book more directly involved a dog in the plot, and the publisher decided to put a golden retriever on the cover. And sales went through the roof, or at least my version of a sales roof.

People would e-mail me with the same message: they loved the book, but were embarrassed to say that they bought it only because of the dog on the cover. That was fine with me; I wouldn't have cared if they'd bought it because the Devil made them do it, as long as they bought it and liked it.

Pleased with the spike in sales, the publisher prevailed

upon me to write another "Andy," though persuading me was not exactly a tough hill to climb. I love working on those books; when I start a new one, writing the ensemble cast makes me feel like I'm reconnecting with old friends. As long as people keep reading them, I'll keep writing them.

A couple of weeks later, the publisher sent me a mock-up of the book jacket for the next one, even before I had come up with a plot concept.

It had two dogs on the cover.

A Bernese and a golden.

So I wrote the book, *New Tricks,* to the jacket. I've got a hunch Hemingway never worked like that. But I didn't care; people were buying the books.

It will come as no surprise that every "Andy" since then has had a dog on the cover, and I'd be very surprised if any of the future ones do not.

I am crazy about dogs, but I'm not above using them to make a profit.

You know the old saying "You only exploit the ones you love."

Jenny

Since I got into rescue, I seem to attract distraught women. Before I got into rescue, I attracted almost no women, but that's a longer story.

This particular distraught woman was named Mary, and her family had two dogs, Ben and Jenny. Ben was a golden retriever and Jenny a smallish Lab mix, and Mary and her family, which consisted of a husband and two small kids, couldn't keep them.

Circumstances were forcing them out of their home and into an apartment, where the dogs were not allowed. So they had set out to find good homes for their dogs. They would place them only together, since the dogs were buddies, and we completely understood that.

The dogs were young, maybe two or three years old, and therefore added a significant amount of energy to the house.

Our house is rarely lacking in canine energy, so it was an adjustment, more for us than for them.

They were the two fastest dogs I had ever seen, and both handled a tennis ball like Roger Federer. And they were great friends not only with each other but with the other dogs as well.

Ben died prematurely at the age of six, the victim of cancer. Cancer in goldens is a horrible problem; if you walk into a vet oncologist's office, half of the practice is golden retrievers.

Jenny is ageless, just as active and lightning fast as the day we got her. She could jump over any fence we might use to contain her, but she has no reason to. She's no dummy.

She's also supremely, annoyingly affectionate. Like most of the dogs, she'll come over to be cuddled but simply cannot get close enough. She literally sleeps on my pillow at night, and I've woken up many times with her tongue licking my ear. I don't recommend that to anyone.

Jenny is epileptic, but her seizures are infrequent and mild. She is going to live forever, which is fine with me.

Disaster

I had no idea where we were stopping, probably somewhere in eastern Colorado. It sort of didn't matter, since every place looked the same. Especially at that point, since it was eleven o'clock at night.

We stopped for gas, and then drove about half a mile to a huge grass and dirt field. Far off in the distance were highways seemingly surrounding the place, but it wasn't too noisy, and we could walk the dogs without interference.

Because it was secluded, and because the dogs were not having a meal at this stop, we decided that rather than set up the fencing, we were going to walk them on leashes. It was the second time we'd done this, and we were pretty good at it.

We took them off one RV at a time. I put a leash on each one, and then helped them down the steps to one of our team waiting to walk them. When they'd done what they had to do, we loaded them back on and went on to the next RV. It sounds methodical and overly careful, and it probably was, but it felt like the only way we could be in total control of things.

I had neglected to bring choke chains, which was not very bright of me. While the name sounds cruel and punitive, choke chains are the proper devices to use when walking dogs. This is especially true of our dogs, most of which are not used to being walked on a leash. But since I hadn't brought chokers, we attached the leashes directly to each dog's regular collar.

Mary Lynn was walking Jenny, a smallish Lab mix who is mostly black, with white markings. She is by far the quickest and most agile dog we have, and one of the smartest. She's amazingly fast, and can jump higher than any dog I've ever seen.

Suddenly, and I have no idea how it happened, Mary Lynn was no longer walking Jenny. Instead, she had somehow escaped the leash.

Mary Lynn screamed, and by the time I looked over, there was no sign of Jenny. She had taken off running at high speed into the darkness, off in the direction of a highway that had to be half a mile away. It was a distance that Jenny could cover very, very quickly.

So we spent a full minute staring into the darkness, screaming "JENNY!" There was some highway noise around us, and I couldn't imagine she was still close enough to hear us, but we kept yelling.

This wasn't the worst nightmare I could foresee for this trip, but it was close. I had no idea what we could do. We certainly couldn't just continue on our merry way, leaving her behind. We would never see her again; maybe no one would ever see her again.

It was even worse than if a dog was to get sick and needed to be hospitalized. In that case we could find a vet and leave the ill dog there. Then we could fly back whenever it was well enough to come home.

But this left us paralyzed, and the possibilities for dealing with it were not very appealing. We could load all of the dogs into two RVs, leaving one of them behind with a few people to search. Or we could leave one person behind, who could follow in a rented car if Jenny was found.

We were all stunned. The entire purpose of the trip was to care for these dogs, and even though it was nobody's fault (except mine for forgetting the choke collars), we would always look back on the trip as a tragic failure.

The only positive aspect to this was that before we left, Debbie painstakingly prepared all new collars and tags, with our new contact information, for the dogs to wear. They had our Maine address and my cell phone number. It was a small consolation, but at least if Jenny was found, the person finding her would know whom to call.

There was nothing to do in the moment except begin walking in the direction that Jenny had run. I didn't know what we could accomplish, but Erik and I started doing so. The others would stay behind, to take care of the dogs that we hadn't lost.

And then suddenly I thought I saw some motion in the distance, and a few seconds later, Jenny went by us, a blur in the night. She headed straight for the closed door of the RV that she'd been riding in and started scratching at it, panting heavily but with a big smile on her face. She'd had a great adventure, but it was time to go home.

Everybody surrounded her, petting her, and someone attached another leash to her collar. But it wasn't necessary; Jenny had no intention of running away. Been there, done that. She just wanted to get back with her friends, and Debbie opened the door and let her in.

Apparently, Jenny was enjoying the trip a hell of a lot more than I was.

The incident had left everybody shaken and had cost us more than an hour. We were all tired, and nobody was eager to spend another night trying to sleep on the vehicles. We asked the GPS to find us a nearby hotel, and fortunately there were a couple of them only six miles away.

We drove there, and the first one we reached had a NO VA-CANCY *sign up in front. If it was full, it must have been cheap; this was not exactly a Four Seasons we're talking about. Fortunately, the second one was nicer and had vacancies, so we parked in the rear of their parking lot, and Debbie and I went into the office.*

We rented six rooms for eight people, since Joe and Terri would obviously share a room, as would Erik and Nick. We made plans to get together at six o'clock in the morning. That would give us five hours sleep, or I should say it would give them five hours sleep. Emmit, Debbie, and I would stay on the RVs, since there was no way we could leave the dogs alone. Any sleep we got would be a bonus.

I finally fell asleep for a couple of hours, and then reluctantly made the rounds at six o'clock. I was amazed at how everybody once again got up eager and ready to go. They claimed to be looking forward to the new day, even though it promised to be pretty much like the old day, which had not exactly been a barrel of laughs.

Cyndi Flores reported that it took a couple of hours for the room she was in to stop shaking, but she finally realized it was just the residual effect of being on the RV for so long.

I tipped the person at the front desk, and we all took turns taking showers in the rooms, then had coffee in the lobby. Once we'd accomplished this and were feeling human, we walked and fed the dogs, and we were back on the road by about seven thirty.

There was no way we were going to stick to our original schedule, so I called ahead and moved the room reservations in Maine back a day. The people at Damariscotta Lake Farm were completely amenable to the change, amazingly so since the five rooms we were taking represented all the rooms in their hotel.

Then I adjusted the flight reservations for people to get back home, a process that I expected to be a hassle, but which turned out not to be very difficult at all. When I was finished, all the flights were rescheduled for Saturday, and unless something went very wrong, we would definitely make it.

I hoped it would be the only time we'd have to make these changes. Jenny, for her part, promised not to cause any more problems.

Tommy and the Snake

One of the many awful aspects of the Katrina disaster was the effect on the animals in the New Orleans area. I doubt that anyone can forget the heart-wrenching stories of people being rescued but then being told that they could not take their pets with them. Many, many animals died in the storm and its aftermath, and a great many more were never reunited with their owners.

Rescue groups from all over the country descended on the area to provide assistance, and California groups were at the forefront. Dogs were brought back to California and other states to be placed in homes, a fact that I had mixed emotions about.

There was no question that these animals deserved to be saved, but the truth is that animal rescue, especially in California, is a zero-sum game. The number of homes willing to take in dogs is far less than the number of dogs needing those homes, so when one dog is rescued, another isn't.

So I wasn't entirely comfortable with the time and effort spent to put the Katrina dogs in a priority position, while just as worthy dogs already in California were being put down by the thousands. I understood and approved of the motivation, but it seemed unfair.

Nevertheless, when another group called us and asked us to take a small golden mix from the Katrina area, we did so. Nobody knew his name, and we called him Tommy. Tommy was less than forty pounds, probably eight years old, and in pretty good shape physically.

As in all adoptions of Katrina dogs, we had to agree that if the owner ever turned up and was searching for Tommy, we would give him back. We obviously had no problem with that, but it never happened. I always felt bad about that, because Tommy was a well-cared-for dog and must have had an owner or owners who loved him.

So Tommy joined the crew without a hitch. It was amazing, and it happened almost every time; after fifteen minutes, you could never tell which dog was the new one. They just seemed to blend in and be accepted by the group. It was nice to see Tommy, who had been through so much, living such a peaceful, safe existence.

One evening about six months after we got him, Tommy wasn't around at dinnertime, a very unusual occurrence. I went out on the property to look for him and saw him coming up the path to the house. He seemed a little unsteady on his feet, but not too bad, and I walked back with him.

I tried to feed him when we got there, but he had no interest. He was also drooling, something I had never seen him do before, and when I went to wipe it off, I noticed that his neck was swollen.

Our vet's office was closed, so I rushed Tommy to an emergency hospital, and they immediately knew what had happened: he had been bitten by a rattlesnake. Debbie and I knew that there were rattlesnakes in the area, but we had never seen one on our property. I hadn't noticed the small marks on Tommy's face. He must have seen the snake and went over to check it out, only to get bitten in the process.

It was touch-and-go for a while, and it took six vials of antivenin and intense treatment over three weeks, but Tommy made it. He had been through a rough time before getting to us, and now a rougher time once he was here, but he was a fighter.

Tommy lived another two years, during which time he was healthy and apparently happy.

Two weeks after Tommy was bitten, I heard shrieks coming from our driveway. Our mobile dog groomer, Sofia, who was parked in our driveway bathing a dog, had seen a snake sitting on the pavement. Apparently, she was not a fan of snakes, something she and I had in common.

She was hysterical and couldn't even tell me what was going on. She pointed to it, which was enough. It looked like a baby rattler, though it was hard to tell since it was curled up. I had heard from our vet that babies were the most dangerous, but it wouldn't have mattered if it were Great-grandpa Rattler and took its dentures out at night. I wasn't going anywhere near it.

"Any chance you'll kill it?" I asked, not holding out any hope for a positive response. I didn't get one, so I cut a deal with her. I would kill the snake if she would agree to then take it out of the driveway.

She signed on to the plan, albeit reluctantly. I think she only went along with it because she would need to go past the snake to get to her truck, and she was not about to do that if it was alive.

Since I had previously been panicked about being in that same driveway with a dead coyote, a live snake just about gave me a stroke. But I had no choice; I had to do what I had to do.

I am David Rosenfelt, the great snake hunter.

I had a few possible approaches: I could go after it with a knife, or chop off its head with a shovel, or drop a large rock on it. Each of these would have required great courage in the face of danger, so instead I drove my SUV over it.

That didn't kill it.

It just pissed it off.

Not only that, but it reacted by moving over, so that it was only a foot or so from the side of the house, too close for me to drive over it again. We were at an impasse and I wanted to declare it a draw, but I couldn't. To leave the snake alive and in place was to invite the possibility that another of our dogs would get bitten.

We had a strip of wood in our garage, at least fifteen feet long, a leftover from some construction that had been done. I took the wood and moved, actually inched, toward the snake, which was waiting for me. It was probably my imagination, but it seemed to be actually sneering its disdain. Apparently, it had researched my history in situations that required some level of bravery.

I got the wood up against the snake and nudged it out a couple of feet toward the middle of the driveway. I then dropped the wood, got back in the car, and did another drive-over. This time it appeared to do the trick, and after jostling the snake with the wood a bunch more times to confirm that it wasn't moving, I told the groomer that she could go ahead and get rid of it.

She refused, just out and out reneged on our deal. What were the odds that I would find an even bigger coward than me? You can throw a dart out your window and be sure of hitting someone with more courage than me. But she had the practical upper hand, if not the moral one. It was my driveway, so it was more important to me to get rid of the dead snake than it was to her.

I finally hit on a reasonable and fair solution. I took our power washer out of the garage and hooked it up, and the groomer hosed the snake out of the driveway. She knocked it out onto the road outside the driveway, to a place where I wouldn't have to get close to it.

So it just lay there, dead.

But it was gone the next day.

I did not want to know where it went or how it got there.

Heathcliff

As I've said, we generally don't take dogs from owners, since our view is that those dogs have their owners to protect them, while dogs in shelters do not. But sometimes we make exceptions, especially for golden retrievers, and it's most often because of the story that the owner tells us.

Debbie took a call from a woman who had two dogs, a golden named Cathy and a black Lab named Heathcliff, both of whom were seniors. She explained that her long-existing allergies had worsened, and she could no longer keep Cathy. Heathcliff, having shorter hair, presented less of a problem, and she was going to keep him.

Debbie could tell how much this woman loved the dogs, and how much pain she was experiencing in having to do this. So we took Cathy, an absolutely wonderful dog, and the woman visited her occasionally, for short periods at a time.

Cathy died after a couple of years with us, and about a year

The Puppy Express

after that, the woman called and asked us to take Heathcliff. He was ill with arthritis and Cushing's disease, and she was having difficulty caring for him and affording the expensive medication.

When we got Heathcliff, he was in bad shape and was having great difficulty walking. But the meds that our vet put him on led to a very significant turnaround, and he maintained an excellent quality of life for two years. He handled the trip on the RV like a trouper; he was one of the dogs I worried about for what turned out to be no good reason.

Heathcliff died in his sleep a few months after we arrived in Maine. He was one of the few dogs we had whose previous owner we knew, so we knew that he was loved for his entire life.

That is a very comforting thing to know.

That Lying Calendar

It simply was not possible that it was only Wednesday morning, which meant it was less than forty hours since our Monday evening departure. Based on my infallible body clock, we'd been in the RVs for a little over three years, give or take a decade.

It was just more of the same, and the same hadn't exactly been a barrel of laughs. Feed the dogs, stop for gas, walk the dogs, stop for gas, ad infinitum. Each time we stopped, the people from the other RVs regaled me with funny stories about what a great time they were having.

Of course the stories didn't seem all that funny to me. Mostly the people were getting a kick out of how the dogs climbed all over them, or how they woke up with dog hair in their faces. It was basically the kind of thing that's happened to me every day for the last eighteen years.

I can tell you from experience . . . once you get past the first decade or so, the dog-hair-in-the-face thing can lose its charm.

In any event, I didn't need our team members to tell me what a grand adventure this was; I kept reading about it on Facebook.

Nebraska went on forever, and it didn't seem to serve any particular purpose other than to aggravate me. Were I the ruler of the empire, I would have broken it into about four hundred states the size of New Jersey. That way it would have given us the illusion that we were getting somewhere.

Tollbooths were a bit of a hassle. We went through back-to-back, and I paid for all three RVs to save time. But this was tricky, in that we had to avoid allowing any cars to get between us. Although I certainly couldn't see why they'd want to.

Emmit was finally willing to give up the driver's seat again, if only for a short time. Erik was taking over, and I was going to lie down on the bed in the back to get some sleep.

That was wishful thinking; it was like sleeping in a pinball machine. I was getting thrown from side to side, which I admit would have been worse if there weren't wall-to-wall dogs on the bed with me to cushion the impact. But sleep was simply not going to happen.

I got up and staggered to the front, and I quickly saw that the reason I was getting thrown around was that we were swerving all over the road. I heard Erik say to Emmit, "You'd better take over," and Emmit was not arguing the point. So Erik pulled into the next rest area and got up.

"What happened?" I asked.

He shook his head. "I'm just not comfortable with the steering."

This was not a positive development. First of all, Erik was a terrific driver, someone we'd been counting on to handle a lot of the load. Second, he had generously offered to take the vehicle back to Virginia after we arrived in Maine. If he couldn't do it, then I'd have to. I had been counting the minutes until I could permanently get off that thing, and now I was going to have to drive it by myself for another full day. And it would be a Saturday; while the world was watching college football, I'd be taking the stupid thing to Virginia.

But it was what it was, and there was no getting around it. Handling the steering was a fairly important part of driving, and if Erik was having a problem with it, then he shouldn't be behind the wheel. It was also understandable; having driven the same RV, I can attest to the fact that it was not easy. I was just glad Erik was honest enough to admit it.

Emmit got back behind the wheel, and I took my customary spot in the passenger seat. I was resigned to the fact that I was never going to sleep again in this lifetime.

The dogs had caught on to the fact that when we stopped, they'd have a chance to get off the RVs and run around. Unfortunately, since we stopped so frequently for gas, they were growing more insistent, and we felt guilty about their being cooped up, so we'd let them off.

This was a time-consuming process, even though we were getting better at setting up the fence. Wanda the mastiff made things even more complicated that morning by walking right through the fence. Wanda could have walked through the Great Wall of China, so a flimsy plastic fence was no problem at all.

Fortunately, Wanda doesn't possess Jenny's speed; she's more of a lumberer. Nor did she have any desire to run away; the RVs were where the food was, and Wanda makes it a habit to stay in close proximity to food. But I still had to retrieve her and reset the fence, both of which took time.

At one point Terri told me that we were fifty miles away from being halfway to Maine. She said that as if it was good news; but as a country-half-empty person, I wasn't thrilled.

"Any chance the next half is shorter?" I asked, but she didn't think so.

Cyndi Flores had been using her iPad to scout out locations for us to stop for dog feeding times. I have no idea how she did this; I can barely play Words with Friends on mine. But she looked at maps or something, and called to say that we could stop at a certain exit. Then her RV would take the lead and bring us to a place that afforded us lots of space and no bystanders to distract the dogs.

This time we were about an hour from Iowa City and it was getting late. She announced that she had the perfect place, and we got off the highway. She then led us along a road for at least fifteen minutes. I had no idea where she was going, and I was starting to think that she didn't either.

But wherever it was couldn't be good, since for every mile we spent off the highway, it was another mile we'd have to cover going back.

Finally we found ourselves on a small dirt road that seemed to lead up a sloping hill. At the top of the hill, the setting sun was shining brightly into our faces as we drove.

Technically it was a dirt road, but it really should have been called a dust road. As Cyndi's RV drove on it, it sent up a dust cloud so thick that it was completely blinding. It was almost like we were in a blizzard; the already lightly colored dust was further illuminated by the sun, and we literally couldn't see through the whiteness.

I called Cyndi to find out what the hell was going on, but there was no cell service in the area. This was no surprise; it was so desolate that I doubted they even had electricity or running water.

Since by now I was driving completely blind, I stopped, and I hoped that Joe behind me could see us well enough that he would avoid smashing into us. He did; Joe had stopped as well, no doubt for the same reason as we did. I waited until Cyndi had gone far enough ahead of us that the dust from her vehicle wouldn't impact us, so I could then set out again to follow her.

Joe and I got out to discuss the matter. We couldn't reach Cyndi, who was by now off in the distance and apparently not looking back. So there was really nothing else to do but continue to follow her. Maybe we'd reach the top of the road and there below us would be the Emerald City.

There was only one home on the road, a small farmhouse that was set back at least fifty yards. As I went by, I saw the door open and a man standing there, looking out at us. He was a very large man; I thought he was going to have to bend down to come through the door, and a second later I realized that I was right, because he exited the house.

In his pajamas.

We continued on up the hill, and through the mirror I could see the man walking toward the pickup truck in front of the house. I hoped he was going down the hill to the market or something, but I had my doubts.

Cyndi was stopped at the top of the hill, and Joe and I pulled up right behind her. It was a dead end; her iPad had let her down. The only way out of there was to go back down the hill, and it wouldn't be easy to turn the vehicles around in that area.

Worse yet, the guy from the house was heading toward us in his pickup. He might well be pissed that we'd invaded his space with these huge vehicles and blown dust all over his property.

I hoped he didn't have a gun with him, but having seen Deliverance, I preferred a gun to a banjo.

Emmit, Erik, and I got out of our RV, and a few other people did so as well. I assumed my customary position near the back of the group, a general directing his troops from the rear.

"Where you all going?" the guy asked, a big smile on his face. He seemed so pleasant that I made my way toward the front.

"Well, we don't actually know," I said, and a conversation ensued about where we were, where we wanted to go, and the best way to get there. We all avoided asking him why he was in his pajamas while it was still daylight. I'd never been in Iowa before; maybe they weren't considered pajamas there. Maybe it was his bowling team uniform.

He heard the barking from the vehicles and thought the story was hilarious when we explained to him what was going on. He was still laughing when he got back in his truck and headed back to his house; because he lived in seclusion out here, this might well have been his first contact with certified lunatics.

We gave Cyndi's iPad another chance, and this time it came through, bringing us to a park not too far from the highway where we could do the feeding and the walking. It was getting dark, so we hurried things along. In our "dog park," it was way better to be able to see where we were walking.

Once again we made the decision that we should not drive all the way through the night but should instead find a hotel, and we went online and found one not far past Iowa City. We called ahead and reserved six rooms.

Debbie, Emmit, and I would again sleep on the RVs with the dogs, while the others would stay in the hotel. It had gotten quite cold, so I got Emmit to show Debbie and me how to work the heater.

It was going to be another long night.

Dogs Can Bring Us Together

My pre-writing career, as I mentioned earlier, was in movie marketing, and my last job in that field was with Tri-Star Pictures, where I eventually held the title of president of marketing. It's an understatement to say that my career was not exactly filled with huge hits; I probably buried more movies than anyone in the history of Hollywood.

There is almost always a natural tension between filmmakers and the movie studio, especially the marketing people. It is understandable; when you include the development of the property, the shooting of the film, the postproduction and editing, et cetera, the directors have often put two years of their lives into making a movie. They want desperately for it to succeed, since that is how they will be judged, so they pressure the studio to spend whatever is necessary to make the film a hit.

The studio executives, of course, have to worry about the bottom line. So they make judgments as to the film's potential, and spend accordingly. The filmmaker, if dissatisfied with the budget or perhaps the creative material or even the pattern of release, will frequently blame the studio for the film's eventual demise. He might just be frustrated or he might be right.

One of the earlier films that we released at Tri-Star was *Short Circuit,* a fairly entertaining film starring Steve Guttenberg, Ally Sheedy, and Fisher Stevens. It was directed by John Badham, who had previously had commercial and artistic successes including *Saturday Night Fever* and *War Games.*

The plot revolved around a robot, named Number Five, that had been developed as a military weapon. Struck by lightning, the robot improbably became "alive," with human intelligence and emotion, and was soon renamed Johnny Five. Then it was up to Guttenberg, the unlikely and miscast inventor of the robot, and Sheedy to save it from the villains of the film.

This was not a movie that would go down in the annals of great filmmaking, and it wouldn't change anyone's life. But people liked it, and it did decent business at the box office. I've had worse, believe me.

A couple of years later, our production people decided to make a sequel. It would be done on a relatively small budget, and it was felt that the favorable reaction to the first film, increased by subsequent viewings on cable and VHS, would be enough to let us realize a profit on the sequel. It was almost entirely a business decision, not a creative one.

As frequently happened in situations like this, the original players were not interested in reprising their roles. Only Fisher Stevens signed on; Guttenberg and Sheedy were replaced by Michael McKean and Cynthia Gibb.

John Badham also chose not to direct, and he was replaced by Ken Johnson. Ken had enjoyed a successful career in television, most notably on *The Incredible Hulk* and *The Six Million Dollar Man*, and now he was trying to make his mark on the big screen.

The result, in my view, was a slight, amusing movie that did not reflect the quality or uniqueness of its predecessor. It was inevitable; the screenplay was mediocre at best.

More significant, my view was shared by the people above me, the ones who made the important decisions. So our financial support for the film was not overwhelming. We didn't completely abandon it, but we didn't treat it like anything close to a potential blockbuster.

Therefore, the relationship that Ken Johnson and I had was fairly contentious. He wanted me to do more, but it was outside my power to do so, even if I had thought that would have been the right thing. Marketing people are definitely limited in their ability to exercise influence and make important decisions, which explains the joke that was told with annoying frequency: "Did you hear about the idiot actress trying to make it in the business? She slept with the head of marketing."

The combination of a less-than-inspired movie and the tepid support we gave it resulted in a very weak box-office performance. The film was quickly out of the theaters, and Ken was openly resentful about what he felt was the short shrift given to his work. He had done as well as he could with a weak script and an average cast, but it hadn't been enough. So I didn't blame him for being upset, even if I didn't agree with him.

Nine years later, the Tara Foundation, which meant Debbie and me, got a call from a woman named Susan Johnson, who was looking to adopt one of our golden retrievers. As I always did, I spoke with her at length over the phone, to tentatively determine whether she would provide the kind of home we would allow one of our dogs to go to.

She sounded terrific, and we made a plan for her to come to the vet facility with her husband that Saturday. They would meet the dog, a four-year-old named Parker, take him for a walk, fill out an application, and hopefully fall in love.

As I'm certain you realize by now, Susan's husband was Ken Johnson, whom I hadn't seen or spoken to in almost ten years. He was as surprised as I was, and it felt more than a little awkward. Our only prior experience together was my viewing him as a thorn in my side and his viewing me as someone who potentially damaged his career.

So we talked very little about the movie and a great deal about dogs. And what Debbie and I discovered was that Ken and Susan Johnson were wonderful people who shared our love for dogs in general, and golden retrievers in particular. Theirs was as great a "dog home" as any we'd ever encountered, and we encountered a lot of them.

Parker, the dog they adopted, was a phenomenal golden, and it was love at first sight for the Johnsons. They took him without hesitation, and for a couple of years they would send us pictures of him lying on their couch, swimming in their pool, et cetera. It was the perfect adoption; the kind of matching of dog with humans that makes us feel completely and totally rewarded for our efforts.

Then we got the horrible phone call: Parker had contracted cancer, and he'd died. The Johnsons had had him for only two years; he had passed away at the ridiculously young age of six. I know there are many people who believe that everything happens for a reason, but there is no reason for golden retrievers to die so young.

The Johnsons got another dog, because that's what people like that do. And I'm sure they loved him, maybe even as much as they loved Parker. If there were more people like Ken and Susan Johnson around, rescue groups would be unnecessary.

But I tell the story because Parker, just by being Parker, had the power to get Ken and me past whatever problems we'd had in the past. Speaking for myself, I looked at him in an entirely different light, one I wish I had the benefit of all those years before.

Thanks, Parker.

Little Sara

Debbie and I were in Phoenix visiting friends one day when we got a call from a rescue person in Orange County asking if we could take a chocolate Lab that was in the Orange County shelter. His name was Hershey, and he was ten years old.

Hershey had been found as a stray and brought in by animal control. Amazingly, despite his advanced years, he was successfully adopted out, but he'd been returned. The people reported that he barked constantly and they just couldn't handle it, or at least didn't want to. Of course, he could bark constantly in our house and we probably wouldn't notice.

If there is one thing that guarantees demise in one of these shelters, it's being placed and returned. Because Hershey now had that big strike against him, and considering his advanced age, the rescue person keeping an eye on him was sure that his time was about up. So she called us.

We drove back from Phoenix, and what I should have

done was drop Debbie off at home before heading to the shelter. But I wasn't thinking, so I brought her with me.

When we got to the shelter, we went into the office to tell them that we wanted to take Hershey. At least I thought we went into the office together; when I turned toward Debbie, she was nowhere to be found. As ominous developments go, that was a beauty.

I realized at that point that she had gone to the kennels to check for other dogs that might catch her eye. This was at a time when we were no longer actively placing dogs in homes, so any she came up with were by definition going to join our clan.

She came up with only one additional dog, a ten-year-old beagle named Sara that had been turned in by her owners. She had already been at the shelter for three weeks, an inordinately long time, and she sat in her dog run like the queen of England. Other dogs come to the edge of the cage to lick hands and otherwise try to curry favor with potential adopters, but not Sara. Her look let us know that if we were going to take her, it would be on her terms.

So we went home with Hershey and "Little Sara," thus dubbed because we already had a Bernese mountain dog named Sarah. At that point we had approximately thirty dogs at an average weight of maybe eighty-five pounds, so we are talking about well over a ton of dogs. Yet Little Sara, all thirty-five pounds of her, immediately dominated them all, and does to this day.

The house was her private kingdom. If another dog was on a particular chair, Sara walked over and proceeded to bark and stare them down. I was included in her general disdain; if I tried to get her off the chair so I could sit down, I got a threatening growl.

Only Debbie escaped her wrath, and Sara's favorite place was on the back of the couch just behind Debbie's neck. I think she also liked that spot because the height gave her a chance to look down upon her subjects.

Sara had a craving for chicken soup that bordered on the maniacal. I swear, she went nuts if she so much as saw a can of it. If we ever cooked any, she would simply not let us alone until we gave her a bowl of it. And then another.

Sara is the only dog ever to get off our property in Orange County. Debbie noticed she was missing on a Memorial Day morning, and when I walked around the property looking for her, I noticed that the gardener had left a gate slightly ajar. Sara was the only dog we had—one of the few dogs we've ever had—that could have fit through it.

We lived in the canyons on the top of a hill, which is to say we lived in the middle of nowhere. Very often at night we would hear coyotes cackling, which I'm told meant that they were in the process of making a kill.

The idea that Little Sara was out there, fending for herself, was driving Debbie and me crazy. We searched for hours, with no luck. To make matters worse, the shelters were closed because of the holiday, so there was no way to determine if perhaps she had been found and taken there.

It was starting to get toward evening, and we were panicked. Finally Debbie came up with an idea that would have seemed insane to anyone but me. I went to the market and bought at least a dozen cans of chicken soup and brought them home.

Debbie poured the soup into two containers, and we drove off in our car, each of us holding the soup out the window. We would drive a hundred feet or so, and then stop, giving the aroma a chance to spread out. It seemed ridiculous, but there were no neighbors around to watch us, and we knew enough about Sara to apply the *Field of Dreams* line to the situation: "If she smells it, she will come."

And she did.

I almost still can't believe it to this day, but she came walking out of the brush—sauntering, really—as if she didn't have a care in the world.

Debbie got in the backseat with her container of soup, and I lifted Sara in. She didn't need any coaxing, and within moments she was slurping away.

We got her home, and she took some water, then headed straight for her favorite chair. She didn't stop to chat with any of her friends, who I'm sure must have been at least a little curious about her adventure. Within a very short time she was asleep, and so were we.

I think we had a much rougher day than she did.

As I'm writing this, Little Sara is almost fifteen years old, as obnoxious and adorable as ever. She likes the chairs and chicken soup in Maine a lot.

Back to Basic

I was in college during the Vietnam War and faced the very real possibility that I would be drafted when I graduated. My patriotism was so strong that I wanted to protect my nation's army from having me be a part of it, so I joined the reserves. Unlike now, reservists at this time were rarely called up to active duty, so my joining effectively ensured I would not be shot at.

Reservists have to go through basic training, and they do so with members of the regular army. I took basic at Fort Leonard Wood, Missouri, in the winter, and it was so cold that one day when my unit went out for target practice at the rifle range, the first guy to shoot had his skin stick to the trigger. I spent those eight weeks frozen and miserable, complaining constantly to anyone dumb enough to listen.

I was a barrel of laughs even in those days.

The worst part of all, and there were plenty of bad parts, was going out on bivouac, which is essentially camping with sergeants yelling at you. Camping under the best of circumstances is not really my thing; showers and indoor plumbing have always held more of an appeal for me. So I can vividly recall, even all these years later, the nights spent on bivouac, and how awful it felt.

And there, outside Iowa City, those memories all came flooding back to me. It was five o'clock in the morning, and I felt like I was back in the army. I was lying in the upper bed in the RV, wearing underwear and covered by just a thin sheet. It was freezing; according to weather.com on my phone it was twenty-five degrees, but it felt even colder. Actually, it didn't feel colder in my extremities, because I was so cold I couldn't feel my extremities.

I'd left the heat running overnight, as Emmit had instructed, but either it had stopped or it was the worst heater in the history of heaters. I considered getting up to look at it, except there was no possibility I could fix it, and I might wake the dogs.

The dogs were sound asleep and therefore very quiet. The only sound I could hear was a rattling noise, but I figured that was my teeth.

It's fascinating how times like that can put things into perspective. Here I had thought I was miserable the previous night, but this was teaching me that I'd had no idea what true misery really was. It was comforting in a way, knowing that I had finally reached a sort of nirvana of wretchedness. I was at the bottom of the hill of depression, and the only way out was to follow the dusty dirt road up.

I was not only freezing but cringing. Any minute the dogs were going to start to bark, and I would have to get up in the frigid air and deal with them. I dreaded putting on my jeans, because the insides of the legs were going to feel like ice.

We were parked in the rear end of the hotel parking lot, and I was going to have to walk over and wake up the eight members of our group who were in the hotel, warm and comfortable. At that moment I hated those eight people with all my heart.

Once that was accomplished, we would have to feed and walk the dogs. But none of that was going to be necessary until they started to bark, and maybe they wouldn't. Maybe they were as frozen as I was and had just as little desire to face the day. Maybe they'd sleep in until noon, when the warm sun would be shining.

And then it happened. Otis was the traitor that barked first, just once, but in our RV, as in our house, there is no such thing as a lone bark in the night.

I waited ten or fifteen seconds, as the barking built to a crescendo, and then I got up. I couldn't get to my suitcase in the back to get warmer clothing to wear; it was dark and I couldn't see. Besides, we needed to get the dogs to quiet down before the police showed up.

I walked across the parking lot to the hotel. I've had warmer parking-lot moments tailgating at Giants Stadium before January play-off games. It probably took me half an hour, but eventually everybody was up and walking the dogs. I managed to borrow a sweatshirt from Emmit, which provided some relief. Since he was the one who'd set the heater, I briefly considered strangling him with the sweatshirt.

Debbie and Emmit were actually surprised by my discomfort; the heaters worked fine in their RVs, and they'd both had relatively comfortable nights. Because of that, I added them to the list of people that I hated.

I was getting a little worried that I was running out of Pill Pockets. Pill Pockets are small, cylindrical items that have a hole carved out of the middle so that pills can be inserted in them. They look like chocolate, though they are obviously not, since chocolate can be very dangerous for dogs.

But dogs love these things, and they make pill-giving far easier than it otherwise would be. And in our house that's not an insignificant matter. We've got more arthritis sufferers than the average Florida retirement community, and between them and the epileptics, I give out in excess of sixty pills a day. I thought I might have misjudged the amount of Pill Pockets we had to bring along, and if that turned out to be the case, it might require a time-consuming stop at a PetSmart.

But I am nothing if not quick on my feet, so for dogs that were taking multiple pills, I just doubled up and put two pills in each pocket. If the Donner party had shown that kind of resourcefulness, they'd be chowing down at Smith & Wollensky right now.

We'd figured that we were about two days away, which in dog-trip time meant another year and a half. But we were close enough to calculate when we would make it to Maine, and after consulting with the others, I estimated we could be there by late Friday afternoon.

I made sure the bed-and-breakfast was confirmed for Friday night, and did the same for the Saturday plane reservations. Everything was as it should be, at least for the moment.

Randy, Joe, and Emmit figured out why I had no heat in the RV. It had less than a quarter of a tank of fuel, and the heater automatically shuts off at that point to conserve the remainder. It was good that they knew that, because if it had happened again the next night, the coroner would have been able to put the cause on my death certificate.

So within a few minutes we were back on the road. Yippee-skippee.

Dogs and Ducks Don't Mix

The previous owner of our house in Orange County was an animal lover. Not a maniac like us, but he was right up there, and he certainly surrounded himself with a substantial collection of nonhumans. He had four dogs, three cats, and six ducks. The ducks were housed in an open-air sanctuary, fenced in, with a man-made pond in the center that emptied and refilled automatically.

He explained to us that while he was taking the dogs and cats with him to his new residence, there was simply no place there for the ducks to live. His request was that we keep and take care of them.

Debbie was, of course, fine with it. She would have been fine if he were offering us a herd of pet giraffes. But I'm not really a duck guy, and I had enough "stuff" to clean up. My view changed when the guy told us that various people had offered to take the ducks off his hands, but they all planned to eat them.

It is no fun cleaning up a duck area. Believe me when I tell you that a dustpan and broom will not do the trick. You know what bird droppings are like? Well, this was as if the birds were a squadron of B-52s.

But I did it. Not as often as I should have, but I did it. My weapon of choice was a high-powered hose, and the ducks were smart enough to move out of the way when I got to work.

Then, one day, one of the ducks didn't get out of the way. He just sat there, which worried me. I could not get him to move. He also did not look good, and I decided that he was sick.

I couldn't call our vet; it was Sunday and the office was closed. I found another vet in Anaheim, and I had to cajole the receptionist to fit me and the duck in. I may have exaggerated the ailment; I said the poor thing could not move, though it's possible that was true. It certainly wouldn't move for me. But the receptionist said they were very busy, so I wanted to make sure we got in.

I folded a blanket and put it at the bottom of a carton. I went out to get the duck, which didn't please me. I don't like touching animals other than dogs and cats. And I don't think I had actually ever touched a duck in my life whose first name wasn't Peking.

But I got him in the carton, carried it to the car, and set off. We didn't talk much on the way to the vet, which was fine. As man-duck relationships went, ours had never been particularly close, and I was a little bitter, because there were NFL games on that I was missing.

I pulled up in front of the vet hospital and went into the office, holding the carton with the duck in front of me, its head over the rim as he checked out the surroundings. There was a roomful of people in the reception area, all of whom looked up at us as we came in. It's not often that you see a duck enter a room. I put the carton on the floor; ducks are heavier than you might think.

For some reason the vet was behind the reception desk, and when she saw me, she said, "Is that the duck that can't move?" I said that it was, and she said, "Let's take a look."

She came over, kneeled down to the carton, and took the duck out, placing him on the reception area floor. The poor, paralyzed duck then uttered a single quack and proceeded to run across the room to the reception desk, leaving a trail of diarrhea along the entire route.

"Say hallelujah," I said. "It's a miracle."

That was a fun duck day compared to one time when I got home from the supermarket. As always, the dogs greeted me with a modest level of enthusiasm when I arrived. Debbie got mobbed whenever she came home; I was always greeted somewhat more cordially.

One of the goldens, named Gypsy, seemed particularly excited. She also was soaking wet—strange since it was the summer, which meant it hadn't rained in more than four months.

It took me a moment to run through the possibilities. I could come up with only one, and it was a disaster to contemplate. I ran outside onto the property and out to the duck sanctuary.

Sure enough, the door had somehow opened, and dogs had gotten inside. There were three dogs in there when I arrived, two goldens and a German shepherd named Rudy. I assume more had been inside—certainly the still wet Gypsy had been—but they must have left to see me when they heard me pull up in the car.

I quickly locked the cage behind me, so that the other dogs

could not get in. The two goldens were on the cement, barking at the ducks, but surprisingly not willing to jump in the pond. Rudy had no such reservations; he was in the water and chasing after the ducks. There was nothing friendly about his attitude; for Rudy it was duck-hunting season.

I ushered the two goldens out of the sanctuary, all the while screaming, "RUDY! RUDY!" I saw him look up at me, but his expression wasn't saying, "Oh, sorry, Dave; I'll be right out." Instead he was saying, "You want me to leave? Are you crazy? These are ducks we're talking about. I've been waiting my whole life for this."

I couldn't reach Rudy, and he was closing in on the ducks. Eventually he was going to get one. The thought of watching Rudy kill a duck was even more horrifying than getting in the pond, as disgusting as that was.

So I jumped in.

Actually, "jumped" isn't the best description. I waded in, moaning audibly at the fact that I was literally swimming in duck shit. I headed toward Rudy, who seemed so surprised to see me that he didn't bother to resist. Which was fortunate, because if I'd had to stay in there an extra minute, I would have first killed him and then myself.

Finally I got him out of the sanctuary and locked it behind me. I then ripped off my clothes and threw them out.

It was early August when I got into the shower, and probably mid-October when I got out.

A Moment of Weakness

It could be that I was getting delirious, but it was at our first stop that morning that I experienced a sentimental moment. Sentimental moments for me come along about as frequently as Mets World Series wins, and I'm always surprised when I suddenly have one.

This one came as I was walking Weasel along the perimeter of our makeshift dog park. I looked over at all the great dogs milling around or lying down, and it hit me that pretty much every one of them would have been dead had we not intervened.

And then there were the people, these selfless, amazing people who'd given up their lives for a week to come do this. I knew they were having a great time, even if I had no idea why, but by any standard this trip had not been a walk in the park . . . it was more a tiring tiptoe through the dog shit.

And then there was Debbie, who at that moment was hugging Bernie and Louis simultaneously. If she didn't exist, I wouldn't have gotten involved in dog rescue. But if I didn't exist, she would still have devoted herself to it.

I would love her no matter what, whether her time was spent saving dogs or collecting stamps. She takes her passion and runs with it, and a good strategy is not to get in her way. I can feel intensely about things as well, but I'm usually passionate from a seat on my recliner, remote control resting on my chest.

The way Debbie immersed herself in dog rescue was remarkable, and it's not an emotionally easy thing to do. In baseball, they say a hitter can make it to the Hall of Fame by hitting not much more than three hundred, which means succeeding three out of ten times. But dog rescue is a hell of a lot harder; there is simply no chance to save three out of every ten dogs in Southern California shelters. For that reason it can be incredibly frustrating, and it can burn you out very quickly.

Debbie just shrugged this off and pushed on, using her time and money and energy and whatever else was necessary. The love and caring she put into the process over all the years makes me love her that much more.

And I looked at Wanda the mastiff, a gentle, lovable giant. There are thousands of Wandas chained up in backyards, spending their days alone and without the human contact they crave. I was just glad and very grateful that we had enabled her to live such a great life.

And of course there was Weasel, lumbering slowly at the end of my leash. Weasel had been with us since the beginning, which was almost seventeen years before. She'd lived with us in Santa Monica and Orange County, and since she had slowed down markedly, I'd been nervously hoping she'd be around to live with us in Maine.

And I decided that she would, even if I had to carry her across the finish line myself.

I remembered when we decided that Weasel would become a member of our family. She was the first dog for whom we had a permanent tag ceremony.

Some couples might play games like "lonely housewife and handsome deliveryman." Not Debbie and me; our playacting, like everything else in our lives, is dog related.

So I would pretend not to want a dog that we'd brought in to become a permanent member of the household, and Debbie would pretend to try to convince me, though she was never successful. But she would "secretly" order a permanent tag, and once that arrived, the rule of the game was that it was too late for me to protest. So we'd gather all the dogs around and conduct a ceremony in which we'd put the permanent tag on the new dog.

I know . . . not exactly "stranded driver and the farmer's daughter," but we liked it. And the dogs liked it when they all got a biscuit as part of the ceremony.

But the goofiest thing I do, which I've never told anyone but Debbie before, is I talk to the dogs. Not just hanging out, "how's it going" conversations, and it doesn't happen that often, only when there's something of significance to discuss.

For instance, whenever we bring a new dog into the house, I talk to the newcomer just before I go to sleep. It's usually comfortably ensconced in a chair by then, or lying on one of the twelve thousand dog beds we have lying around the house.

But it had to have had a rough day, coming into a house with maybe thirty dogs, all of whom had bombarded the new one with attention and curiosity. And much worse than that is probably the life the new dog led before us that resulted in its being dumped in an awful shelter.

I never have any way of knowing how much it has been bounced around, or how many times it has been abandoned or thrown out.

The poor dog could be viewing our house as just one more stop, one more place in which it would ultimately not be wanted.

So I would lean down and spend a few minutes petting and telling the dog that it was safe now, and would be comfortable and loved forever. I'd say how happy we were that it was part of the family, and that it should just relax and enjoy life. The dog never responded verbally, but I would keep petting until it shut its eyes, so if there was any discomfort it was well hidden.

The other time I'd talk to the dogs was when they were ill and we both knew the end was near. I'd tell them that I knew they didn't feel well and that we wouldn't let them feel that way for much longer. I'd tell them not to worry, that we would do only what was best for them. And I'd tell them that it was great having them as part of our family and that we would always see them that way.

But at that moment, in that makeshift dog park next to the RVs, I leaned down to talk to Weasel. We'd had a lot of conversations over the years. "Weasel, old girl, we've come a long way."

She didn't answer me, which was to be expected. Weasel had never been much of a conversationalist.

"You're going to love Maine," I said. "We're on a lake, and the last time we were there, wild turkeys came right up to the house." The truth was I had no idea whether Weasel had feelings for wild turkeys, either positive or negative. I was just very happy she was going to live long enough to see them.

Debbie came walking toward us; I would have bet everything I owned that she knew exactly what I was feeling.

When she reached us, she leaned down to pet Weasel and then looked up at me. "She's going to make it," Debbie said.

I nodded but didn't say anything, since I was in the process of experiencing another sentimental moment. It was the second one in a half hour, doubling my previous high.

Finally I said, "Yup."

I'm at my most eloquent in sentimental moments.

Feeding Time at Home

One of the difficulties of having so many dogs is the fact that they like to eat.

Every day.

Day after day.

Vets say that it's best for dogs to be fed twice a day, so that's what we do. It's not easy, and each feeding takes probably forty-five minutes or so, depending on how many dogs we have at the particular time. But it is truly something to behold.

The dishes are spread out all over the house, and each dog knows exactly where his or her dish is going to be. Some of them inhale their food and then go on the prowl to find those who they know are not going to finish. Others just hang out with their food, not showing any interest at all until I start to pick up the dishes, at which point they spring into eating action.

We separate from the group those that might be on special

diets for reasons of health. They go into rooms by themselves, behind closed doors, to eat in peace.

The only one to always be separated not for reasons of health is Wanda, the mastiff. After a month or so of her chowing down on everyone else's food, we started putting her in the laundry room, separated by a half door, open at the top. When she'd finish she'd stand with her head at the open area, looking down at the others eating, wishing she could have their food.

But Wanda couldn't get to them; and she wasn't happy about it. At times I thought she was going to eat the door.

In ten years at our house in Orange County, I don't think there were three occasions, outside of Thanksgiving and Christmas, that Debbie and I ate at a table.

It was just too much of a hassle. First of all, once any food was put on the table, it then had to be guarded. Therefore, one of us would have to bring all the courses in while the other stayed vigilant. Wanda, for instance, would need about thirty seconds to clear off and suck down the entire meal.

The eating itself was no easier. Dogs would completely surround us, pleading looks on their faces, wanting some of our food. Then, of course, there were the non-silent beggars, barking angrily at not being invited to dine at the people table.

Of course, Debbie would make it worse by slipping some of them tastes of the food. Very rarely did they react by barking, "OK. Thanks for that . . . enjoy the rest of your meal." Instead it obviously got them even more eager for even more food, and pissed off the ones that hadn't had a sample.

It wasn't an atmosphere conducive to fine dining, and as you can imagine, we didn't throw a hell of a lot of dinner parties. Instead we ate standing up, in the kitchen.

In addition to the dogs' meals, there were other things we did that could best be described as unusual. We used to get two dozen bagels each morning, and the dogs would surround us in the kitchen. Debbie and I would break up the bagels into bite-sized pieces and drop them into the waiting mouths of the dogs.

But on Thanksgiving and Christmas, we would up the ante. We'd buy a half-dozen large London broils and cook them on the grill. That was the easy part; it was the cutting of the meat that was hard. Because of that experience, if there was a London-broil-cutting competition in the Olympics, I could go for the gold.

It would take two or three hours from beginning to end, but each dog wound up with a dishful of meat, and not a single piece went uneaten.

Ever.

I used to imagine that at London broil time, veteran dogs in the house probably nodded to the newcomers that had never experienced it and knowingly barked, "I told you so. Is this a cool place, or what?"

Liza

Liza is a big, burly golden retriever that we got from Lorie Armbruster, a good friend and a great rescue volunteer in Orange County. Liza was a victim of some kind of hoarding situation. I sometimes think that we might be considered hoarders, though I suppose a major distinction is that hoarded animals are not well cared for or loved; they are simply kept.

Liza's pretty much a loner; she's happiest when she's in her own space. For a long time that space was in the bathroom, in front of the toilet. I think she liked the cool floor, but it definitely made for a few awkward moments.

Liza has a really thick coat, and after we were in Maine for a while, we noticed a small amount of blood seeping through it on her back. It turned out that she had a cyst underneath the coat, and therefore not visible. It had ruptured—hence the blood.

Our vet performed the minor surgery required, and he had to shave a good deal of her hair in the process. We decided to finish the job and had our groomer shave her the rest of the way. It was the beginning of summer, and everyone felt that she would be more comfortable.

Her reaction was immediate and weird. She was no longer interested in staying in the bathroom, and in fact became much more sociable. She started climbing up onto one of the recliner chairs, an act that at her age and weight I never thought she could manage.

Now, with Liza and Kahlani constantly stationed on the two recliners in the TV area, Debbie and I don't watch as much TV as we used to.

Go East, My Friends

I've always preferred the East to the West. My experiences are limited to living in New York or New Jersey on the one end and California on the other, so I realize I'm making way too broad a generalization. But people in the East seem realer and friendlier and a hell of a lot less pretentious. Plus, there is actual weather in the East; the years are divided up into four seasons.

Pretty much the only upside to California is the fact that NFL games start at ten in the morning, and nighttime football is finished by nine at night. Staying up until midnight or later to watch was going to be difficult, especially for the first couple of years, since I figured it would take that long to catch up on the sleep I was missing on the RV.

But the trip provided another reason for preferring the East; the states are narrower. We could get through them quicker. The Nebraskas of the world take forever to cross, and there is not even the illusion of progress. Once we got past the Mississippi, the fact that we were able to cross states off our list more rapidly made me feel like we were approaching the home stretch.

I got an e-mail from George Kentris, a Taco Bell franchisee in the Findlay, Ohio, area and a good friend of Debbie's and mine. He'd been following our progress on Facebook, as had apparently most of the free world. George was wondering if we'd be coming through the Findlay area, because he'd very much like to house and feed us if we were.

This was an offer with some teeth in it. In addition to owning Taco Bells, George owns a couple of Comfort Suites hotels, and he said that we could stay there overnight, or just use the facilities to shower and get refreshed.

I consulted Cyndi Flores, our official navigator, and she said that if we stayed on schedule, we would pass right by Findlay at around six P.M. And the hotel that George was offering was no more than three minutes from the highway, so stopping there wouldn't set us back much at all. That's about as perfect as it gets, so I e-mailed George and told him to expect us.

We got to Findlay right on time, and what was waiting for us felt absolutely fantastic. The Comfort Suites hotel was right across the street from one of George's Taco Bells, and we parked behind the hotel. There was a large grass field in which we set up the dog fence so that we could walk and feed the dogs.

There were signs up at the hotel welcoming "Woofabago," and George had his whole staff there to meet us and provide whatever help we needed. They absolutely could not have been nicer, and we could not have been more grateful.

George gave us the keys to a bunch of rooms in the hotel, and we went in to shower. It was the single best shower I had ever taken, and it was the first time I'd felt human in what seemed like months. I even took fresh clothes out of my suitcase that did not have dog hair on them, which would be a short-lived state of affairs.

Once that was done, George led us over to the Taco Bell, where our gang ordered whatever they wanted, free of charge. This particular store was serving as a test restaurant for the Doritos Locos Tacos, so we got to sample it before the rest of America.

Of course, as good as the food was, the people in our group had already made it clear that they would rather eat dirt than the food I had stocked the vehicles with. I used this opportunity to throw most of it out, since the refrigerators were not great, and the cold cuts didn't seem to be aging well.

We took advantage of George's hospitality for at least two hours. I know that a shower and a bunch of tacos may not sound like a dream vacation, but I cannot tell you how much I and the rest of our gang appreciated all that George had done.

He had been incredibly welcoming and provided the best two hours of the trip. Of course, as far as I was concerned, there weren't too many other hours competing for that honor. But Debbie and I were extraordinarily grateful for George's generosity and hospitality, and always will be.

In fact, since he's a huge Ohio State fan, I find myself rooting for the Buckeyes in his honor. He's also a Browns fan, but I'm not quite ready to go that far. I mean, all we're talking about is a shower and some tacos, right?

I had the fleeting idea that I should hide in a hotel bathroom in the hope that the others wouldn't notice and the RVs would leave without me. I opted not to, figuring that if I'd come that far, I could make it the rest of the way. Besides, Emmit would realize what I was doing and rat me out.

It's fifteen hours from Findlay to our house in Maine, so we drove for five hours and then stopped to get some sleep. Nobody felt the need to find a hotel; we'd just catch a few hours on the vehicles. Then we'd get an early start in the morning and drive straight through.

We pulled the RVs into a park, walked the dogs, and settled in for some sleep. It made me a little nervous when we did this; if local police decided to check out three strange RVs, there was no telling how they'd react to what they found inside. We weren't doing anything wrong or breaking any laws, but it was conceivable they would have had us committed and institutionalized.

But there were no incidents, and when I woke everybody up at six A.M., for the last time, they were all raring to go. We walked and fed the dogs, and pulled out.

I couldn't believe it myself, but this was the final leg. Even I was feeling invigorated.

Slightly.

Please, Please Don't Kill the Dog

There are certain consistent themes, questions, and reactions I get in my e-mails from readers providing feedback for my books. One of them is "I saw your picture on the book jacket. How did you get so tall and handsome?" Another is "You make Shakespeare look like a hack."

These are, of course, all part of my elaborate fantasy life. But the actual comment I really get most frequently is "Please don't ever kill Tara."

Readers tell me that they turn to the end of the book and scan it to make sure that they still see Tara's name, which provides reassurance that she doesn't die during the book. This fear extends to any other dog characters I include, and doesn't deal only with death. No one, and I mean no one, wants a dog to suffer so much as a hangnail.

Debbie and I are the same way. If we see a dog or other

animal as part of a TV spot or trailer for a film, we seek reassurance from someone who has already seen it to make sure the animal emerges unscathed. Humans can die by the boatload, but if a dog is hurt or wounded, the film is off our list.

I once got a manuscript from an agent asking me to read a client's upcoming novel, in the hope that I would like it and give them a quote to use on the jacket. I agreed, and since it was the first time I had ever been asked, I was flattered.

I actually flatter pretty easily, and in this case, even if the novel read like the Manhattan telephone directory, I would have praised it as a "taut and gripping winner." So I started reading it, and on page twenty the bad guys were trying to get information from the protagonist.

When he resisted, they didn't torture him.

They tortured his cat.

There is almost nothing else that could have been in the book that would have prevented me from giving a favorable quote. But in this case I just couldn't do something that might cause other people to read about cat torture. So I stopped reading, called the agent, and apologized.

But when it comes to my own books, Tara's existence and circumstances present a bit of a dilemma for me. The Andy Carpenter books are chronological; that just happened naturally, and it seems fair to the reader. So hopefully characters evolve, and they certainly get older.

Except for Tara.

In the first book, *Open and Shut,* Andy says that Tara is seven, and that he rescued her when she was two years old from a shelter. Seven is well into middle age for a golden, as ridiculously unfair and stupid as that might seem. Their average life expectancy is twelve, and that doesn't take into consideration how cancer-prone they are.

The books have come out once a year since then, and the current one, *Unleashed,* is the eleventh. In that book, Andy mentions that Tara is nine.

Perhaps you notice some mathematical problems with all of this. Tara should be seventeen.

But she's not, and she's never going to be. Andy's Tara is going to be nine for as many books as I write. Andy could be in a home sucking oatmeal through a straw, and a nine-year-old Tara will be by his side. He'll take nine-year-old Tara to AARP meetings. I may even move her back to seven, if the mood strikes me.

Debbie and I decided long ago that we were going to keep the memory of the original Tara alive for at least as long as we were around. I feel that we certainly did that with the Tara Foundation, and we're doing it to a lesser degree in my books.

So when readers write to me, I tell them the absolute truth. They don't have to skim ahead in the book to see if Andy's Tara gets hurt or gets sick or dies.

Because in this instance I am all-powerful, and I have decreed that a happy and healthy Tara will live forever.

Snickers

If there is such a thing as a well-intentioned, caring scam, then that's how we got Snickers.

A young woman called us one day about eight years ago, tearful about a situation she was facing. She was in college at Cal State Long Beach, and spent her free hours rescuing dogs and finding them homes. It's a very difficult thing for someone without an established organization to do, and she was unhappily discovering that.

The bottom line was that she had rescued a dog, Pandy, from certain death, and had nowhere to put her. She was out of options, and the only one remaining, to bring Pandy back to that shelter, was too horrible for her to contemplate. Would we take her?

I said that we would, and I arranged to meet the woman in a parking lot in Anaheim. When I arrived, I saw Pandy in the back of her SUV, along with Charlie and Tiger and Coco and

Snickers. The woman told me that she couldn't bring herself to tell me over the phone that there were five dogs, because she knew I would turn her down.

She got that right.

But they were all seniors, and all were targeted for euthanasia, and she just couldn't bear to see it happen. None were purebreds; they were all dyed-in-the-wool mutts, and all adorable.

I have no idea why, but I took all five. I also gave her a lecture on how full we were in our house, and said that we would not be taking any more dogs from her. She seemed fine with that; maybe she had other suckers lined up.

Of course, as always happens in situations like this, the dogs turned out to be great. I am aware that I describe every dog as great or wonderful, but that's because dogs are great and wonderful.

All of them lived for at least three years, but none made it to five, except for Snickers, who is still going strong. There's a look about him that makes it impossible to tell his age; he doesn't look much older than he did when we got him. But obviously, back then he wasn't a senior.

So Snickers made it to Maine, and his thick coat makes this the perfect place for him. He joins Bernie outside when it starts to snow.

"Welcome to Maine"

That's what the sign said, and within seconds Cindy Spodek Dickey had a picture of it up on the Web. It meant that we were just a little more than two hours away, or at least two hours in driving time. In dog hours, that's about a month.

The truth was we were making good time, and the only negative thing to happen that morning was a tray of blueberries and strawberries fell out of one of the refrigerators and onto Snickers. Mary Lynn cleaned him up as best she could, and we didn't miss a beat.

We stopped near Kennebunkport to set up our dog park one final time. Neither George nor Barbara Bush was there to greet us, which obviously meant that Charlton Heston hadn't put in a good word for me after he adopted Willie, the chow mix.

It was an uneventful stop, unless you viewed the first meal the dogs would ever eat in Maine sentimentally. I didn't, nor did I tear up over the fact that it was the first time they would ever use Maine as a bathroom.

Our next stop was the Portland airport, to drop off Erik and Nick. They were actually renting a car and driving back to California; I think it was going to be a sightseeing, father-son bonding trip. I could have been imagining this, but when they got off, I think it was with some disappointment that they wouldn't get to be there when we arrived at our destination.

I thanked them profusely; they were very helpful and enjoyable to be with, excellent members of the team.

Pulling up to the airport curb with three RVs is a tricky maneuver, as the Portland airport is small and the road is narrow. I couldn't even imagine what airport security must have been thinking as they observed us, but nobody stopped us.

The best way to our house is to get off the highway in Brunswick and take Route 1 north. It takes us through towns like Topsham, Bath, and Wiscasset, and I had to admit that I was getting excited. Driving through these towns helped to hit home just how much I love it up there.

With the RVs, it was more difficult to navigate roads like these than highways, so I let Emmit stay behind the wheel. He'd probably driven 70 percent of the way, but amazingly seemed fresh and had maintained his cheerfulness.

Debbie and I exchanged text messages about how great it felt to finally be there, and how much we were looking forward to seeing how the house had turned out. We hadn't been there in over a month, and back then it still looked like a construction site. I trusted that the contractors had done a great job, but it was going to be nice to "trust and verify."

We hit some traffic just before getting onto the Wiscasset Bridge.

It's not uncommon, because there is always a crowd of people at a place called Red's Eats, which sells lobster rolls from a small shack. It is amazing, but there is never a time when the place is not mobbed, and the lines have always discouraged us from trying it. It reminds me of the old Yogi Berra line about a restaurant, "Nobody goes there anymore; it's too crowded."

But then we were about fifteen minutes away, passing through the wonderful town of Damariscotta. I spread the word through text messages to the rest of the team that when we all pulled up in front of the house, Debbie and I wanted to go inside to see the place first, when it was in relatively pristine condition.

It would be the only time that we would ever see it without its being filled with dogs and dog hair, and we wanted a chance to savor the few moments of solitude and cleanliness. We also wanted to see everything before it was destroyed by the house's canine residents.

We came to a dirt road, and Emmit commented on how rural the area seemed. I assured him that the next road we would take made that one look like Route 80. We made the turn onto that road, and then into the long unpaved driveway that leads to our house.

We are in an incredibly beautiful area, ten acres of wooded land on a lake. Living there was going to be like waking up every morning in a Folgers commercial. It seemed amazingly serene and quiet as we pulled up, the last time that would ever be the case.

There are no neighbors within barking distance, which was a requirement during our house hunt. We didn't want to have to spread borax in the forest, or create beaches outside, or worry that the noise was bothering neighbors.

Debbie and I got out of the RV, as did Emmit, Cindy Spodek Dickey, and a couple of others. We went into the house, and it was everything we could have hoped for. Hervochon Construction did a great job; all that we asked for had been accomplished, and then some.

I'm a huge Giants fan, a fact that I pointed out to the contractors in great detail while torturing them about the Super Bowl victory over their beloved and previously undefeated Patriots. So they'd responded by filling the place with Patriots paraphernalia; there was a Patriots schedule on the refrigerator, a Patriots toothbrush in the bathroom, a Patriots jersey hanging in the closet. Mainers are apparently very bitter people.

We went back outside and I shared the plan; we would bring the dogs to the outside, fenced-in area that the doggie door leads to. It would be the easiest way to do it from the RVs, with the least chance that dogs would get away.

We started to shuttle them in, and the process took about forty-five minutes. Once we did, we opened the door and they were able to go into the house. It was fun to watch them experience their new surroundings; less so to watch a couple of them "mark" the occasion. But a house isn't a house until it's been pissed in.

Emmit's wife, Deb, had flown up from Atlanta to meet him, and they would be staying with us for a day and then exploring Maine a bit. I left them in the house with Debbie and the dogs, and then I took our car and led the RV caravan to the bed-and-breakfast, Damariscotta Lake Farm. As we were learning, everybody knows everyone else in these small towns, and we had heard about the place from our electrician, who is the owner's brother.

Once again we were the beneficiaries of terrific hospitality, and there were signs welcoming "Woofabago." I told everyone that Debbie and I would be back in an hour for a group dinner, and I headed home, although I was not yet thinking of it as "home." This time when I pulled up there was somewhat less quiet and serenity;

the barking was so loud that I was sure our California neighbors could hear it.

We got ready for dinner and headed back over to Damariscotta Lake Farm to meet the group. We were a little nervous leaving all the dogs in a strange house; by the time we got home they might have dismantled the place and sold it for scrap.

It turned out that there was a full restaurant at the hotel, and we had a table for ten in the center of it. It was a quiet, very comfortable place, and I'm sure all the other patrons could hear every word of Debbie's very moving toast.

"You didn't just help us get here," Debbie said. "You did it with a smile, and you made it fun." She talked about what we'd been through, and how amazing each and every one of these people was to have put their lives and sanity on hold to help us.

Then she stood up, held her glass in the air, and announced to everyone in the place, "Please toast the greatest people on the planet." And everyone in the restaurant applauded, raised their glasses, and drank.

The food and atmosphere in the restaurant was wonderful, and I was sure we would be coming here a lot. Even the check was wonderful, half of what it would be for a New York or Los Angeles restaurant, with the food every bit as good.

I was going to like it here.

Looks Can Be Deceiving

I got an e-mail from a reader in Maryland once, asking me if by any chance I knew of a golden retriever rescue organization in Orange County, California. She had heard about a golden in the Orange County shelter that was in terrible physical shape and facing euthanasia.

She sent me a link to the shelter's Web site, with a picture of the dog, which the shelter had named Junior. It was a tiny, grainy photo, and it was impossible to tell what the dog looked like. But I could see enough to know that the poor thing was miserable.

I have no idea if the reader really knew where I lived and was being disingenuous or if it was a coincidence, but it didn't matter. We lived about a half hour from the shelter, and Debbie and I went down there to take a look and get the dog.

Unfortunately, even the taking a look part wasn't going to be easy. Junior was not in an area that the general public had

access to; he was in the medical ward. So we went to the counter and told the woman behind the desk that we wanted to
adopt Junior, and we gave her his impound number.

She looked him up on the computer and then conferred
with an associate. Then she went in the back and didn't reap-
pear for at least ten minutes. There was clearly an issue with
Junior.

When she came back, she told us that Junior was ill, and
that it was their recommendation that he not be adopted out.
Debbie told her that we appreciated their recommendation,
but that we wanted him anyway. That sent her into the back
again, for a shorter time, and when she returned she said that
their medical officer would speak to us.

Sure enough, he came out a few minutes later and repeated
the mantra that Junior was ill and not a candidate for adoption.

"Is he dead?" I asked.

"No. Of course not."

"Then we want him."

He continued to try and talk us out of it, and I asked what
was wrong with Junior. He told me that he had tumors all over
his body and a horrible skin condition that could never be
cured.

"What's the condition?" Debbie asked.

"We haven't determined that."

"Then how do you know it can't be cured?"

The truth was that they were never going to determine it,
and certainly they would never try to cure it. They were going
to keep Junior as a stray for the required five days, and then put
him down. And those five days were up.

Debbie laid out the situation for the medical guy as clearly as she could. We would adopt Junior and take him to our vet. If our vet determined that Junior could not be made to have a good quality of life, then we would put him down, holding and petting him during the process. If he could fix what was ailing Junior, then we would have him do so, whatever the cost.

Either way, we were not walking out of the shelter without Junior.

They brought him out, and I don't think I have ever seen a dog look worse. He had at least four obvious tumors on his body, including one hanging off his leg that was the size of a grapefruit. He had almost no hair, and his skin was red and irritated. He must have been absolutely miserable.

Of course, if Junior was a golden retriever, then I'm Brad Pitt. He was probably a shepherd mix; we'd have a better idea of that when and if his hair grew back. But a golden he was not.

We took Junior to Dr. Kali at the North Tustin Veterinary Clinic, who is as good as it gets. He took him in the back and spent at least a half hour examining him before coming back with the verdict.

Most of the tumors were just fatty tissue, except the one on his leg. Dr. Kali thought he could remove that fairly easily, and doubted it was malignant. There would be a little difficulty in the healing process, because there would be very little skin to cover the incision. But it would be manageable.

As far as the skin condition was concerned, Junior had the mange. So he would get treated for it, and soon he would not have the mange. He would feel relief almost immediately, and Dr. Kali saw no reason that his hair would not grow back.

Junior, the dog that could not be cured, was going to be fine.

And in fact he was. He was an old dog, but he lived for two years in our house, and I don't think he ever had an uncomfortable day.

The point is, he was going to be discarded simply because of how he looked. The idiots who let him get in that condition in the first place were being unintentionally aided and abetted by people who didn't take the time to find out what was wrong, although the system would not have been prepared to fix it anyway.

I was in the Downey shelter one time and saw a golden mix that the shelter had named Gino. He was young, no more than two years old, which normally would not have made him a likely candidate for us to rescue.

But we took him, because he had bad cut marks on his face. They had healed long ago, and I figured they were the result of a fight with another dog. But they made him look a little angry and intimidating, and in that environment it was extremely unlikely that he would be adopted.

So we took him, and as always our first stop was the vet. He gave Gino a full examination, including the facial cuts, and what he said stunned me.

He showed me that there were similar marks below Gino's jaw. Amazingly, it was not the first time he had seen this condition, and he knew exactly what it meant. Someone had wired Gino's jaw shut so that he could not bark, and Gino's straining against the wires had caused the permanent cuts above and below the jaw.

Ironically, the same cut marks that caused him to be fairly unadoptable now ensured that there would be no shortage of people wanting him. Once he was in our care and we explained to people what had happened, everyone wanted to take Gino and pamper him for the rest of his life.

The most remarkable thing of all was Gino's temperament. What he went through must have been horrible, but he was incredibly happy and friendly. He never stopped smiling, and his tail never stopped wagging.

We found him a great home within the week, and for years after that would get pictures from his owner, with declarations that Gino was the best dog of all time.

Yes, looks can be very deceiving, unless you look really deep.

Please, Not the RV Again

Apparently, dogs don't get jet lag, or RV lag, as the case may be. They woke us up on our first morning in Maine with a barking outburst at a little after five thirty, just as they had in California.

And just as in California, Debbie pretended that she didn't hear them so that I'd get up and do the feeding. Our dogs can awaken people in coffins, but Debbie didn't stir.

I drove over to Damariscotta Lake Farm, where the members of our group who were staying there were having breakfast. The muffins are so good that I would drive an RV to get them, and that's saying a lot. I never want to get into an RV again.

But there the three of them were, sitting in the parking lot. I was driving some people to the airport in my car, Cyndi Flores was driving one of the RVs to Virginia, and Terri and Joe Nigro were driving another one there. That left one, which I was supposed to be in charge of.

I called our contractor, Chris McKenney, and asked him if he knew anyone we could hire to drive the thing down there. I wasn't desperate, but I offered money and my right arm, which was significant, since at the end of that arm is the hand I use to operate the TV remote control.

He found someone. In fact, his brother Dickie was willing to do it. The deal was concluded, and the next day the RV was out of my sight forever.

Two days later, I was driving on the small dirt road not far from our house when I came upon a beautiful white poodle. He was dirty, with small thorns in his coat, as if he'd trudged through some shrubbery. There was a tag on him, but the phone number on it was hard to read. Of all the people to find a stray dog, you'd figure it would be me.

I coaxed him to the car, which did not exactly take a lot of persuasion, and he jumped in. I figured I'd drive him home, and then take steps to find his owner. As I was driving, I passed a woman walking along the side of the road. This is not exactly midtown Manhattan, and pedestrians are in rather short supply.

I thought it was possible that she was out looking for this dog, so I stopped and rolled down the window. "Excuse me," I said, "is there any chance that you're looking for this dog?"

She came over to the window and looked in. "No, sorry. Did you find him?"

"Yes. Any idea who the owner is?"

"No," she said, "but I heard that these dog people moved in down the road."

That was us . . . we were already known as the "dog people."

I took the poodle home, but rather than keep him in the garage for the time being, I decided to bring him into the house. If the other dogs freaked him out, I could always put him in the garage.

So I brought him inside, and he acted like he'd been there all his life. He was a fantastic dog, and I was a little sorry when after a few phone calls I was able to find his owner. He would have made a good addition to the house, because with only twenty-five dogs, it was feeling kind of empty.

But the owners had been frantic about his disappearance, and I was pleased that he obviously had a good home. They had a second dog, and I was sure the poodle would have a bunch of terrific stories to share about his stay with the crazy dog people.

Not long after that, Debbie and I were driving on another road about five miles from our house. This is a more heavily trafficked road, and has a speed limit of fifty miles an hour.

Up ahead we saw what seemed to be another stray dog. He was white, maybe a spaniel mix, and was standing in the middle of the road. We stopped, of course, and Debbie got out of the car. Within ten seconds the dog was in her arms and then in the car.

We couldn't bring him home, since he weighed only about thirty pounds. In our house that would mean the other dogs would pour ketchup on him and have him for lunch. So we found out where the nearest animal shelter was, and we drove there. He didn't have a tag on him, but we were hoping that the shelter could scan him and determine whether he had an implanted chip.

He didn't have a chip, but the people who worked at the shelter were confident that they would find the owner. My strong instinct was not to leave the dog with them; I'd never left a dog at a shelter in my life, and it went against my grain. But they patiently explained to me that this was not Southern California, and that nothing bad was going to happen to this dog.

They promised to call us if they couldn't find the owner, and to notify us when they did. Debbie felt we should leave him there, which was good enough for me. I knew that she would be overprotective, and if she thought it was OK, then I was willing to go along with it.

While I was giving them our contact information, Debbie went into the back and looked in the kennels. She came back with a ten-year-old yellow Lab named Daisy that had been found as a stray. She'd been adopted out once, but returned because of a "raspy bark."

We decided we wanted to take her, and the shelter gave us an application to fill out. One section prompted us to list the names, breeds, and ages of any other pets we might have. I didn't feel like spending a month filling out the application, so I explained our situation to the director of the place.

She seemed to take it in stride, and called both our California and Maine vets to determine that we were for real. Apparently, they gave the OK, because within a few minutes Daisy was our first Maine rescue.

We got her home and introduced her to the crew, and ten minutes after she arrived in the house, she was sacked out on the couch, flat on her back.

Some things never change.

Dorothy, We're Not in California Anymore

If you're an animal, Maine is the place you want to be, except for the part where the people shoot you.

First of all, and I assume this is important to animals that are not domesticated, the land seems plentiful. Unlike in California, where in the summer the only way an animal can find water is by buying Aquafina at the 7-Eleven, there's water everywhere. You throw a rock and you hit a lake.

The woods are lush and filled with stuff to eat. If you like eating grass and shrubs, there's plenty of that. You like eating other animals? This is the place.

And the people that live here are animal lovers. In California, when a workman would come into our house and experience the dogs mobbing him, you could see the panic in his eyes. We would have to put the dogs in rooms, behind closed doors, before most people would even enter.

In Maine, we have workmen here all the time, and they

barely react. It's a totally different mind-set. They think it's funny, and they don't show the slightest hesitation about coming in. Once inside, they spend some time petting and then go about their business. If I walk them out to their pickup truck when they're finished, usually I see a dog sitting on the front seat, waiting patiently.

Of course, the majority of people we've met are hunters. That means they shoot animals with such frequency that the state has to create hunting seasons for each type of animal. Not to do so would mean that so many would get shot, we'd run out of them.

From our Maine house, one can hear gunshots very often, even though hunting is not supposed to be conducted in our area without permission of the homeowners. But everybody here has a gun, except of course for me. Having a gun would scare me to death; I'd keep the gun in the house and the bullets in Connecticut.

The entire situation is counterintuitive, at least to me. How can you love animals and want to shoot them? Now, in fairness, many of the hunters are doing it for the meat, to help feed themselves and their families. But even they seem to enjoy the process; certainly they don't describe it as onerous in any respect. It's a sport to them, and though I'm a sports fan, I just don't get it.

Actually, when it comes to animals, I'm probably a contradiction as well. Obviously I love dogs, but I'm not at all comfortable around many other species.

Soon after we arrived, our contractor came over with his nine-year-old son, Patrick. There was a large turtle out behind our deck, which I was not inclined to go near. Patrick went over to it with a small stick and put the stick near the turtle's face. Suddenly the head and neck shot out and grabbed the stick.

I almost jumped out of my skin, as everyone laughed at me. It turned out that it was a snapping turtle. I didn't even know such things existed; I thought the snapper in snapper soup was the fish.

Of course, my aversion to strange animals pales in comparison to my aversion to bugs, and there are plenty of them here in Maine. To hear locals tell it, the blackflies are so ubiquitous and large, they fly off with small children. And then there are the ticks and the mosquitoes.

So we've taken preventive measures. We have two machines called Mosquito Magnets out in the woods. And we have an exterminator come in monthly to spray for mosquitoes and ticks, and another one to spray for ants, and another to keep away rats and mice. And we put Frontline on the dogs every month to protect them from ticks and fleas, plus we give them periodic injections to ward off Lyme disease.

Except for hiring a Marine battalion to surround the house, we've pretty much done all we can to protect ourselves. Hopefully it will work, because the only other alternative is to move into a biosphere.

In any event, I'm going to stay indoors a lot here.

Epilogue

Today is the one-year anniversary of our arrival in Maine, a fact that has generated a flurry of e-mails from the members of Team Woofabago.

The messages are all the same. Everyone reflects on the grand adventure and recounts anecdotes and feelings from those five days in September 2011. Most notably, and rather bizarrely, they thank Debbie and me for letting them be a part of an event that they will never forget.

It makes me revisit that time and look at it with fresh eyes. Now I can examine it free of stress and worry and judge it by how we felt and what we accomplished. It leads me to one inescapable conclusion.

These people are still nuts.

Maine has been wonderful. I would recommend that everyone move here, except for the fact that one of its primary charms is the lack of crowds and traffic. But the place is beautiful, and the people have been absolutely terrific and totally welcoming to us.

I know I talk in platitudes about Maine, and maybe that will change over time, but right now it's how I feel.

The dogs are doing great. They absolutely love the winter, to the point that it's hard to get them to stay in the house. Bernie the Bernese goes outside when it's snowing, and just lays down. Once he's covered with snow, he gets up, shakes himself off, and lays back down again.

Debbie loves watching them enjoy the snow and the cold. While I certainly share those feelings, I characteristically add a dose of guilt for all the time we kept them in the Southern California heat.

I will forever be grateful to the people who joined us on the trip . . . who volunteered, unasked, to do so. The commitment that they made in terms of time and effort was extraordinary, so much so that as I look back on it, I find it hard to believe. These were adults with real lives, real jobs, and real responsibilities that they put on hold. And in most cases, it was to help people that they barely knew or didn't know at all.

The fact that they did it with a smile, with laughter and confidence, and without apparent friction, only makes it more remarkable. They came together with a seriousness of purpose; they were there to do a job. And they seemed like they were having fun in the process.

Next time I drive twenty-five dogs cross-country, I've got to remember to try that "fun" approach.

At the end of the day, it all came back to the dogs. Had I spread the word that we were moving furniture or vehicles or any other possessions, no one would have stepped forward. Nor should they have.

And they didn't just transport the dogs; they bonded with them and loved them. The e-mails all include references to each person's particular favorites, even remembering nicknames they gave them. The dogs soaked up the love, and I'm sure it made the trip much less stressful for them than it would otherwise have been.

But if I've learned one thing during our descent into dog rescue lunacy, it's that dogs bridge gaps between people. They smooth over the human condition, and they provide an extraordinarily valuable function. They take people of all political persuasions, religious faiths, and geographical locations and represent something that everyone can love.

The value of that really cannot be overstated. The people I have met as I travel the country doing rescue events, as well as the people who have adopted dogs from us, have enriched my life immeasurably. I have no idea whom they vote for, what God they worship, or whether they worship one at all.

And the truth is that I really couldn't care less. There are powerful bonds between us, and they have four paws and shed a lot.

We will not need to rescue prolifically now that we live in Maine. There just isn't a problem here, or anywhere in New England. In fact, homeless dogs are brought up to this area from down South, because here they can be adopted. I don't know if studies have been done about why some places in the United States have animal rescue problems while others don't, but I'm going to look into it.

The overriding point for us personally is that from now on

we won't have to bring in so many; there just isn't the need. Maybe someday we can have a normal life, with a normal number of dogs.

Like fifteen.